# Do You Have Alligator Arms?

# JAMES W. MOORE

# Do You Have Alligator Arms?

## EMBRACING LIFE, HOPE, AND GOD

Abingdon Press
NASHVILLE

# DO YOU HAVE ALLIGATOR ARMS? EMBRACING LIFE, HOPE, AND GOD



*This book is printed on acid-free paper.*

**Library of Congress Cataloging-in-Publication Data**

Moore, James W. (James Wendell), 1938-
Do you have alligator arms? : embracing life, hope, and God / James W. Moore.
p. cm.
ISBN 978-1-4267-1481-8 (trade pbk. : alk. paper)
1. Christian life—Methodist authors. I. Title.
BV4501.3.M657 2011
248.4'876—dc22

2011009905



Scriptures marked KJV are from the King James or Authorized Version of the Bible.

Chapter 4 originally appeared in the Lenten study *The Common People Heard Him Gladly* (Nashville: Abingdon Press, 2003). Used by permission.

11 12 13 14 15 16 17 18 19 20—10 9 8 7 6 5 4 3 2 1
MANUFACTURED IN THE UNITED STATES OF AMERICA

*For the whole gang,*
*June, Jodi, Sarah, Paul, Kirby,*
*Claire, Dawson, Daniel, Mason, Lily*

*and especially for*
*Jeff and Danny,*
*who gave me the idea for this book*

# CONTENTS

# CHAPTER ONE

## Do You Have Alligator Arms?

SCRIPTURE: MARK 10:17-22

*Alligator arms* is a football term often used by coaches, players, or television commentators to describe—and criticize—a would-be receiver who keeps his arms protectively—and timidly—in close to his ribs instead of stretching out full length to catch the ball because he senses a tackler bearing down on him and he is more interested in protecting himself from the hard hit than in catching the ball. The commentator might say something like this: "He's open. The ball is there, but it's off his fingertips, incomplete. Too bad he had alligator arms on that one."

Our son, Jeff, and our son-in-law, Danny, are fun together. Their families live near each other in Dallas, so they are together quite a bit. Whenever they are in the same house, the same car, the same restaurant, the same space (wherever that may be), there is a lot of laughter.

Recently, they were telling me about an experience they had in a fancy restaurant in North Dallas. Some of Jeff's in-laws, Uncle Joe and Aunt Nancy, came to town for a visit. Jeff and his wife, Claire, and Danny and his wife, Jodi (our daughter), decided to take Uncle Joe and Aunt Nancy out to dinner in one of the nicest restaurants in the city. Jeff and Danny knew up front that the meal would be expensive so they agreed to share the expense. However, when the sumptuous meal was over, Jeff and Danny discovered to their surprise that sometime during the meal, Uncle Joe had slipped away from the table, found the waiter discreetly, and paid the bill in full, including the hefty tip. When Jeff and Danny told me about this, teasingly, I said to them: "Do you mean to tell me that you took Uncle Joe and Aunt Nancy out to dinner at this elegant restaurant as your guests, and you let Uncle Joe pay for it?" "O yeah," they said. "We got 'alligator arms'!" "Alligator arms?" I said. "What in the world is that?" Grinning, they said, "That's when the check comes you do this: You pull your arms up tight against your chest and then with short arms like an alligator you say, 'I'll get it! I'll get it!' but you don't really reach out to pick it up and pay the price!"

Now, of course, Jeff and Danny (both former high school and college football wide receivers) were just joking and clowning around with their alligator arms. They fully intended to pay the bill, but the truth is that it's really a pretty common attitude in our world today. Lots of folks today live daily in the spirit of alligator arms. They talk a good game, but they don't really want to pay the price. They want good schools for our children, but they really expect somebody else to take care of that. They want our nation to be strong and good and virtuous and prosperous, but they want somebody else to see to that. They want great churches in our communities, but they are more than glad to let somebody else pick up the tab.

Sadly, this is especially true in the church. People want effective Sunday school classes, creative youth programs, and outstanding music, but they don't want to teach the children or jump on the hayride truck with the youth or sing in the choir. They get alligator arms. They talk big, but they really want somebody else to pay the price.

Now, this alligator-arms attitude is not new. It's as old as the Bible. In fact, that was the Rich Young Ruler's problem. He sort of wanted to follow Jesus, but he got alligator arms and couldn't make the leap of faith, couldn't make the commitment, and couldn't pay the price.

Remember the story with me. Jesus is on his way to Jerusalem, on his way to the cross when the Rich Young Ruler runs up and kneels before Christ. Notice this—"he runs up"—a sign of enthusiasm; "he kneels"—a sign of respect and reverence. So, we can assume here that this young man is not trying to trap Jesus with a loaded question as others tried, but that he is really genuine and sincere when he asks: "Good Teacher, what must I do to inherit eternal life?" Jesus answers, "You know the commandments: Do not kill, do not commit adultery, do not steal, do not bear false witness, do not defraud, honor your parents." Then the young man answers, "All these I have kept from my youth." Jesus then looks at him with love and says to him, "But you lack one thing: Go sell what you have and give it to the poor and you will have treasure in heaven . . . and come follow Me."

At this point the Rich Young Ruler gets alligator arms—he pulls back. He pulls in. He can't bring himself to make that kind of commitment. He can't reach out to Christ and to others, so he turns away and leaves sorrowfully.

Sometimes I think about that story like this: What if a few moments later the Rich Young Ruler had changed his mind and decided to respond in faith and take on the cost of discipleship and follow Jesus? I can see him running back to that place where he had talked to Jesus earlier, to that place where Jesus had invited him to join the disciple group and come along with them and be one of them. I can just see the Rich Young Ruler anxiously and hurriedly running back, only to discover that Jesus and his disciples have already gone. They have moved on, and he missed it. He missed his moment because he got alligator arms. He pulled back, waited too long, and came back too late.

Now, I don't want to sound overly dramatic, but I have found in my experience that this matter of waiting too long, responding too late, refusing to make a commitment, is the stuff tragedies are made of. Let me ask you something: How is it with you right now? Is there something that you have been putting off and putting off? Are you missing out because you just keep waiting around? Is there some commitment you need to make? Some word you need to say, something you need to do? Let me bring this closer to home and be more specific.

## First of All, If You Need to Say, "I Love You"

Don't turn away from that. Don't get alligator arms. I have seen that tragedy happen so many times, people waiting to say, "I love you," somehow never getting around to it, unable to pick up the tab and then suddenly it's too late.

Several years ago, a Catholic priest was serving a parish church and was also the dean of the church's school. He was having a terrible week. Christmas was coming and he felt like Scrooge. The church budget was way down. The school was struggling financially also and might have to close. And people were whispering about his resignation. The priest said he had taken it out on the children all week, stifling their Christmas enthusiasm, sharply criticizing their work, and in general, making life miserable for everybody.

Late one night that week, the priest was working on his Christmas message but was unable to find the words. Finally, he put his pen down and stared out the study window across the snowy schoolyard. In an instant, so quickly it happened—he saw one of his young schoolboys dash into the street chasing a soccer ball. The boy was hit by a car! The priest bolted out of his study, plowed as fast as he could across the snowy yard toward the dying boy. Grabbing him up in his arms, he heard himself saying aloud over and over these words: "Please, please don't die. I haven't told you yet how much I love you."

Your parents, your children, your mates, your brothers and sisters and aunts and uncles and cousins and grandfolks, your coworkers, your neighbors, your classmates, your friends—have you told them how much you love them? Surely you love them, you prize them, you value them, you cherish them, you care for them—but have you told them? Have you told them lately?

It's a great tragedy to go through life and not feel loved. It is also a tragedy to go through life loving people, and yet never telling them. Please don't miss your moment. Please don't wait around or hold back any longer. Please don't procrastinate anymore. If you need to say, "I love you" to someone, don't get alligator arms. Say it today.

### Second, If You Need to Say, "I'm Sorry"

Don't turn away from that. Don't get alligator arms and wait around until it's too late. Some months ago a minister friend of mine was on an airplane flying to Atlanta, Georgia. Seated next to him was a young woman who looked to be in her early thirties. She was softly crying. The minister said to her, "I can see that you're upset. Is there any way I could help you?" She answered, "My father died last night, and I'm on the way to Atlanta for his funeral." "You must have been very close," said the minister. "No," she said, "My father and I have not spoken for fourteen years. I have not seen him since I was eighteen years old. We had a fight, and the last thing I said to my father as I stormed out of the house was, 'I hate you and I wish you were dead.' "

She said, "I didn't mean it. Over the years I have wanted to tell him, 'I'm sorry.' I have thought about it so many times. I didn't mean it. I was an angry, frustrated teenager." Then she said, "My vacation is coming up next month and I had actually called a travel agent to book a flight to Atlanta. I really wanted to set things right with my dad, but now it's too late. I didn't mean it. I didn't mean it when I talked so ugly to him."

Listen! Do you need to say, "I'm sorry" to someone? Do you need to make peace with another person today? Do you need to mend a broken relationship? If so, don't you get alligator arms about that. Don't turn away from that! Don't put it off any longer! Pay the price, swallow your pride, and go do your part. Go fix that. Go right away, and God will go with you.

### Third and Finally, If You Need to Say, "Here I Am, Lord, Send Me"

Don't turn away from that. Don't get alligator arms about that. Say yes to Christ now because there is no better time than right now to make your personal commitment to follow Christ and serve him and go where he leads you.

Years ago a man was in church one day when he dramatically felt the presence of the Lord with him and he powerfully heard the call of God. The man's name was

Isaiah. He "saw the Lord high and lifted up" that day, and he realized as never before how much God wanted him to be God's servant. His response was just the opposite of the Rich Young Ruler's. Isaiah didn't turn away. He didn't pull back or hold back—no alligator arms here. Rather, in faith and commitment, he responded. On the spot, immediately, without hesitation or reservation, Isaiah said, "Here am I, Lord, send me!"

He didn't put it off. He didn't wait around. He didn't look for excuses or try to wiggle out of it. No—in faith and commitment, he gave himself heart and soul to God.

Now, let me be very personal and ask you something: Are you as committed to God as you want to be, as you ought to be? Have you been thinking about joining the church, but putting it off and putting it off? Are you as loyal to God and the church as you could be?

What's holding you back? What are you waiting for? The key is commitment and the time is now! And yet, the truth is that so many of us continue to procrastinate and put off and rationalize and pull back and turn away.

Some years ago Helen Kromer expressed it dramatically in her satirical poem "Use Me, O Lord," which has these words: "I want you to use me, O Lord; / Use me, O Lord, but not just now!" The point is clear and obvious. If you want to give your life to God, if you want to follow Christ, if you want to give your talents, your loyalty, your service to him, then get rid of those alligator arms and do it now—commit to him now. Don't turn away and pull back and wait around, because there is no better time than right now!

# CHAPTER TWO

## Reach Out and Wrap Your Arms around God's Future

SCRIPTURE: 1 CORINTHIANS 13

Each year in January, we celebrate the New Year at our house by cleaning out some things. As we were going through one closet that desperately needed it, we discovered a dusty old magazine that for some reason we had kept for many years. When I saw it, I remembered that we had bought it at the Mid-South Fair in Memphis at one of those classic books and magazines booths.

It was a *Life* magazine printed at the time of the Korean War. On the cover was the dramatic photograph of an American Marine near the front lines of battle. He was a member of the Fifth Company of Marines. His company had originally numbered 18,000 up against

100,000 enemy soldiers. The weather was unbearably cold. The situation was indescribably terrible. The odds against this young Marine and his company were tremendous.

Marguerite Higgins, the Pulitzer-prize winning war correspondent, told of her visit to the front lines the day that picture was taken. It was morning, and the temperature was 42 degrees below zero. Weary soldiers, half-frozen, stood by dirty trucks eating rations from tin cans. This particular Marine was eating cold beans with a trench knife. His clothes were frozen stiff as a board. His face, covered with a heavy beard, was crusted with mud and ice.

His eyes betrayed the weariness of body and spirit and depicted the frustration of daily being matched against the awful threat of hostile weather and a violent enemy. This picture, which had made its way to the cover of *Life* magazine, was snapped just as the young Marine answered a poignant question. The war correspondent had asked him this question: "If I were God and could grant you personally anything you wished, what would you want most of all?" The young Marine stood motionless for a moment, then raised his head and answered: "Give me tomorrow!"

Now, I don't know what happened to that particular young man. I don't know whether or not he got the tomorrow he asked for on this earth. But, I do know this. You and I have our tomorrow we asked for yesterday. And the good news of the Christian faith is that it always offers us a new start, a new chance, a new beginning, a new birth.

But I have discovered something interesting about that. I have noticed that people approach the future and the prospect for change in a variety of ways. Different people see it differently and bring to it a different set of attitudes.

For example, some approach the future with fear and trembling. I've sensed that, haven't you? Some are worried and all tense about the future. They are afraid of what the future may bring. They are uncomfortable in the present, but dread the future even more.

In the play by William Inge called *The Dark at the Top of the Stairs*, a little boy who is eight or ten years old is frightened by the darkness at the top of the stairs. His mother asks him why he is afraid, and he replies, "because you can't see ahead." And that's the problem many folks have as they move into the future. They come to it with fear and trembling, with worry and anxiety because they can't see ahead. And that scares the life out of them.

Others move into the future with despair and pessimism. It's just the same old gray blahs, they think—

nothing to get excited about, just the same old drudgery.

Bertrand Russell expressed this dark pessimism more than seventy years ago when he said: "Life is a long march through the night surrounded by invisible foes, tortured by weariness and pain, toward a goal that few can hope to reach and where no one may tarry long" (from "A Free Man's Worship," *Mysticism and Logic and Other Essays* [New York: Longmans, Green and Co., 1919], 56).

Now, I'm sure that Bertrand Russell was a smart man, and I'm sure he said many brilliant things, but in my opinion, that was not one of them. Because, you see, life is more than drudgery, more than some kind of endurance test. But the truth is, many people see it that way, many people go through life that way, and many people even now are trudging into each tomorrow with an attitude of despair and pessimism.

Now this brings us to another way to move into the future—the way I would like to recommend to us: you and I can step into the future as *believers*.

As people who believe in God.

As people who see history as God's workshop.

As people who believe in the future and who believe the future in!

But the question is how do we do that? How do we

believe the future in? The Apostle Paul helps us here. His amazing letters written to the Corinthian Church some two thousand years ago are in many ways so very relevant for us as we move into the exciting days ahead. In those powerful letters, Paul was making resolutions for the future for the Corinthian Christians! He was wiping the slate clean and giving them a new start—and my, oh my—did they ever need a new beginning!

You remember that Paul had started the church in Corinth. He was their founding father, and all had gone so well for a while. But then when Paul had to move on, the church came apart at the seams. Selfishness, arrogance, factions, immorality, cliques, jealousies, and power plays were practically ripping the Corinthian Church to shreds. When Paul heard what was going on, he was disturbed and concerned, so he wrote a series of letters to the church at Corinth to set them straight—and he spoke straight from the shoulder. He laid it on the line. He openly denounced their sinful behavior, their shady business practices, their immoral actions, their feuds and their factions, and then he said, "Let me show you a better way," and he summed up the Christian lifestyle in three powerful words: faith, hope, and love.

In all the confusions and complexities of life, he said, there are three things you can always count on, three things that matter more than anything else, three things (only three) that last forever: faith, hope, and love. And that's what it means to celebrate the present and *believe the future in*, to live each day in the spirit of faith, hope, and love. That's the spiritual formula we need to take with us into the future. Now, let's take a look at these.

## First, There Is Faith

Here is a great approach to the future: In the days to come, I will be a person of faith. That's what it means to believe the future in, meaning to live each day in the spirit of faith in God.

Recently, I traced the word *faith* back into the Hebrew and Greek lexicons to see what the word meant in Biblical times. I found that the word *faith* was used in a variety of ways in Scripture. It meant "trust in God," "dependence upon God," "commitment to God," "confidence in God." The New Testament Greek word for *faith* is "pistis," and it literally means "believing obedience." I like that definition. *Faith* means "believing obedience," believing in God so much that you stake your life on God and devote your life to God.

One day, I was visiting with some children at one of their Sunday school class parties. I asked the children to write down the one thing they could think of that would make our world a better place. I was impressed with their responses. If we will listen, we can learn much from our children.

One child wrote, "Each person should try to be a light in the world and an influence for good."

Another said, "More love and less violence."

Still another wrote, "All people should act like brothers and sisters because after all, we are God's family."

One other said, "Go out and do what you know is right and stand up for what you know is right."

And, finally, one little ten-year-old girl put it bluntly: "Learn the Christian faith and stick to it."

Do you see what the children are saying to us? They are saying, "Live your faith! Practice what you preach! See yourself as God's co-worker in this world."

One of my favorite stories is the one about the well-to-do lawyer from the United States who went on a tour around the world. In Korea, a missionary was showing him around when the lawyer saw something that touched him greatly. An elderly man was out in the fields holding onto the handles of a primitive plow. In front of the plow (where an ox should have been) was the son of the old farmer. The young man was pulling the plow like an ox while the older man was pushing it and guiding it from behind. The lawyer was amazed. He had never seen anything like that.

The missionary said, "Look at them. Aren't they

something? They sold their ox this year so they could give some money toward the building of their new church." The lawyer responded, "My! What a sacrifice!" The missionary said, "No, they don't call it a sacrifice. They call it a privilege! They were glad they had an ox to sell and they are grateful that they are healthy enough and strong enough to pull the plow themselves this year." The missionary paused for a moment and then he said, "You see, they really believe they are working with God!"

Now, let me ask you something:

Do we believe like that?

Do we believe that we are working with God?

Is our faith that strong?

If so, we can believe the future in.

## Second, There Is Hope

Here is another great approach. In the days ahead, I will be a person of hope. To live in the spirit of hope, that's another way to believe the future in. Hope means trusting God now and forever. It means trusting God to always be there for us; to always be with us in every circumstance of life and indeed even beyond this life.

Somewhere I read that among some Native American tribes an interesting rite of passage took place in every little boy's life—a rite designed to help the boy learn the courage of manhood. When he was still quite small, he was taken out into the forest to spend the night alone. Left with nothing but a knife for protection, the little boy was required to remain silent as he awaited whatever horrors the night might bring. The next morning, however, he was greeted with a delightful surprise. He found that his father had been there all along standing and watching all through the night, lest something hurtful should threaten his son. Many of us have discovered something like that in the midst of our own long, dark, and difficult nights. Someone was watching over us all through the night.

Mrs. C. D. Martin wrote a song about this special brand of Christian hope. She had been visiting with a Mr. and Mrs. Doolittle of Elmira, New York. The Doolittles were both physically disabled, but in spite of their difficulties their faith was radiant and their souls were strong. They exuded great joy and spiritual strength. When Mrs. Martin asked Mrs. Doolittle about her inspiring poise and happiness, Mrs. Doolittle smiled warmly, pointed toward heaven, and said, "His eye is on the sparrow, and I know He watches me." Mrs. Martin was so taken by that response that she went home and that very day she arranged those touching words into a powerful Gospel hymn that later Ethel Waters immortalized. "His eye is on the sparrow, and I know He watches me!"

If you and I believe that, if we have that kind of Christian hope, then we can believe the future in.

## Finally, There Is Love

Here is yet another great approach to the future: In the days to come, I will be a person of love.

Some years ago a young law student named William McLaughlin was visiting Chicago for the wedding of his cousin. The bride's father, his uncle, was Dr. Frank Gunsaulus, a prominent minister there. William McLaughlin stopped by the church office to see his uncle. He told his Uncle Frank that he was looking forward to attending church the next morning and hearing him preach. Dr. Gunsaulus gave him a brief preview of the sermon. It was to be about the spirit of Jesus' life—his love, his sacrifice, and his self-giving. The text was "For This Cause Came I into the World. To Love." Dr. Gunsaulus went on to indicate this, too, is our calling, our cause, to love, and to give ourselves for others. With that, William McLaughlin left. As he walked out of the study, he was thinking about that sermon and especially that text "For this cause came I into the world."

As he walked along, suddenly he heard cries and looking up, he saw smoke billowing out of the newly built Iroquois Theatre. The theatre was on fire. What should William McLaughlin do? Should he run away? Should he retreat to safety? Or should he see if he could help? He made the choice and entered the burning building. There he saw panic-stricken people pushing, shoving, screaming, and fleeing from the flames.

Somehow William McLaughlin was able to get up to a balcony door and break it open. He then placed a plank down stretching it across the alley to the safety of the law library on the other side. Quickly, he began helping people across the plank to safety. When all the people were out, he started across the plank, but by now it was on fire. The plank broke and William McLaughlin crashed to the pavement below. Frank Gunsaulus rushed to him. In obvious pain, William told his Uncle Frank that he was thinking about the sermon they had just discussed. He knew that those people up there needed something he could give them. They needed his help. They needed a certain strength he could supply at that moment. Then with his voice straining, William McLaughlin quoted the sermon text, "For this cause came I into the world." He was rushed to the hospital, but his injuries proved fatal. William McLaughlin's last act was one of love, sacrifice, and self-giving.

Faith. Hope. Love. The greatest of these is love! Remember the little first-grader who forgot his birth certificate, and then told his teacher, "I'm sorry but I forgot my excuse for being born!" Faith, hope, love—these are our excuses for being born. Faith, hope, love—these are the ways to believe in the future and to believe the future in. Don't be afraid. Reach out and wrap your arms around God's future.

# CHAPTER THREE

## Reach Out and Wrap Your Arms around Trust in God

SCRIPTURE: EPHESIANS 6:10-17

On my desk in front of me as I write this, I have a small amount of money, United States currency: a penny, a nickel, a dime, a quarter, a one-dollar bill, a ten-dollar bill, and a twenty-dollar bill. And that's about as far as my budget will permit me to go. These instruments of money have a couple of things in common: (1) they won't buy much in today's world, and (2) they bear a common inscription, a common motto that we all know, namely, "In God We Trust."

Now, this motto affirming our nation's trust in God was first placed on U.S. coins in 1864, but this belief was present long before that time. In fact, the theme of trusting God has been a central part of our American heritage from the very beginning. It held our founders together. It motivated them. It inspired them. It undergirded them. It strengthened and encouraged them. They had a dream and a hope. They wanted to build a better life. They wanted freedom. They wanted to forge a new nation in a new land. And somehow they believed that God was with them, that God was in it all!

Have you heard about the little four-year-old girl at the kindergarten open house? There was a patriotic theme and her job that night was to show the visitors a map that she had painted. Proudly she held it up and announced, "This is a map of my country!" Someone in the crowd asked her, "What is the name of your country?" Confidently, the four-year-old answered, " 'Tis of thee! My country 'tis of thee!"

That's a cute story with a profound message in it. That is written large in our magnificent heritage. Our founders believed that. They believed strongly that this country they were shaping was *of God*. They believed that God was with them, moving them, directing them, using them, and they trusted God.

Now, let's be completely honest here. Of course, not all of them felt that way. Some of them acted like anything but children of God—some of them acted like the devil! But for the most part, that is our heritage. Faith and trust in God played a dominant role in the birthing of America. It's our heritage as a nation, and—even more—it's our heritage as a church and as individual Christians: to see ourselves as partners with God working for a better world, trying to do the very best we can, and then trusting God to bring it out right.

The pioneers in the church and in the nation realized that some things have to be left to God. There is a fascinating verse in Paul's letter to the Ephesians that underscores this. In that letter, Paul spends most of the time giving various instructions on the conduct of living the Christian life, and then he closes the letter with these interesting words: "take up the whole armor of God, so that you may be able to withstand on that evil day, and having done everything, to stand firm" (6:13).

Having done everything—stand firm. This was Paul's way of saying that there are some things we can't do anything about except turn them over to God. That is, we do the best we can and then we fall back on God. We build the best foundation we can and then when the storms come, we rely on God. Maybe that is just another way of saying, "In God We Trust."

Now, let me be personal. If we take that phrase, "In God We Trust," and address it directly to ourselves, to our personal lives, what might it mean? What can we entrust to God? What should we entrust to God? Let me suggest a few things. I'm sure you will think of others.

## First, We Can Entrust to God Our Hurts, Our Personal Pains, Our Personal Agonies

Sometimes hurtful things happen in our lives that we can do nothing about except turn them over to God and trust God to bring them out right. Sometimes people or groups or circumstances hurt us, and the gut-level tendency is to get 'em back, to lash out in revenge, to get even. But the counsel of our faith, the message of our Scriptures, and the lesson of our heritage is to stand tall and trust God and to let God correct it and bring healing.

Sam Jones, a famous evangelist of another generation, once got into a fight with the town bully. After the fight, Sam Jones was reminded by someone that the Bible admonishes us to turn the other cheek and Sam, in his characteristic manner, pointed out that he did indeed turn the other cheek and the fellow hit that one, too. Then Jones said, "There being no further instruction from the Lord, I beat the mischief out of him!"

Sometimes we feel like that's what we want to do, but over and over the Scriptures tell us to wait on the Lord, to entrust our hurts to him. There is a verse in the Bible about this where God says, "Vengeance is mine, I will repay" (Hebrews 10:30). Now, as I understand it, this verse is not a commentary on God's wrath or anger. What we really have here is a statement on the futility of bearing grudges or seeking revenge or trying to get even. There is always a kickback in getting even. What this verse is saying to us is leave it to God! Don't give in to vengeance! Revenge is really never sweet—it only leaves a bitter taste in our mouths. Let God handle it and correct it and bring healing. Trust God with your hurts!

Dr. Albert Beaven of Rochester once told the story about a fellow he disliked intensely as a boy. They had argued and fought. There was bad blood between them. Albert Beaven became so infuriated with this other boy that he was obsessed with revenge. Albert Beaven plotted against him. He picked up some of those sticky burrs that fall off bushes and put some of them in his pocket in the hope that sometime he could slip up behind his enemy and grab him, throw him down, jump on top of him, and rub those burrs into that fellow's back. "The trouble was," said Beaven, "the burrs wore my pockets out and scraped my own leg and I was the only fellow to be scratched!"

You see, that's the way it works. The hater suffers more than the hated. How many people today live tormented lives because they are consumed with nursing old hurts and old grievances? How much different life could be for us if we would only remember that justice will ultimately prevail, that the right will ultimately win the day, and that the wrong eventually falls of its own weight.

Recently I saw a bumper sticker that read, "Michelangelo would have made better time with a roller." But, you see, some things can't be rushed. Paul's advice here is helpful. "Having done everything... stand firm" (Ephesians 6:13). That is, do the very best you can, and then trust God. Trust God even with your personal hurts.

## Second, We Can Entrust to God Our Failures; Yes, Even Our Failures

Somehow in the miracle of God's workings, God can take even our weaknesses, even our inadequacies—even our defeats and failures—and use them for good. History proves this over and again.

T. R. Fehrenback's book *Greatness to Spare* (Bridgewater, N.J.: Replica Books, 2000) is a series of biographical sketches of the men who signed the Declaration of Independence. He concluded the book by summarizing what happened to some of those courageous people. Some were imprisoned, some were killed, some were left penniless, some were persecuted, some lost their families, and some received brutal treatment. Their houses were burned. They were called traitors. They were offered immunity and the king's protection if they would recant their signing of the Declaration of Independence, but not one of them—not a single one—defected or changed his stand. I'm sure there were moments when it looked like failure and felt like failure, but somehow God works through our failures and redeems them.

We look back and see Jesus hanging on a cross, and it looks like failure. We see Paul chained in that prison cell, and it looks like failure. We see Lincoln lying on the floor, blood flowing from his head, the victim of an assassin, his work half-done, and it looks like failure. But we know now who the victors were! God can use even what looks like defeat and failure to accomplish a purpose. Isn't that just another way of saying, "Having done everything . . . stand firm" (Ephesians 6:13). In God We Trust. We can trust God with our hurts and our failures.

Remember how the poet put it:

> I asked God for strength that I might achieve,
> I was made weak that I might learn to obey;
> I asked for help that I might do great things,
> I was given infirmity that I might do better things.
> I asked for riches that I might be happy,
> I was given poverty that I might be wise;
> I got nothing I asked for, but everything I hoped for,
> Almost despite myself, my deepest prayer was answered.
> (from "Prayer of an Unknown Confederate Soldier")

## Third and Finally, We Can Entrust to God Our Future

I really suspect that the main thrust of our text is right here. When Paul said, "take up the whole armor of God, so that you may be able to withstand on that evil day, and having done everything... stand firm" (Ephesians 6:13). I think he was trying to encourage those early Christians to not give up, to not weaken in tough times, and to remember that the future belongs to God. If they hadn't been very sure of that, it would have been so easy for them to get discouraged.

Jesus said to them, "Take the gospel to the uttermost parts of the world!" And Caesar said, "If you do, I will kill you!" And he did kill many of them. I'm sure there were times when the future looked dark and bleak and hopeless to them. But Paul had another word, and the word was that God didn't call us to be successful—God called us to be faithful. God didn't call us to bring the harvest—God called us to sow the seed. Paul said, "You do your best! You give it your best shot. You live out your responsibility, now in the present, and leave the future to God!"

This is good counsel for us today in our nation, in our church, and in our own personal lives: do the best you can do now, and trust God for the future. This is what Jesus meant when he said, "strive first for the kingdom of God and his righteousness, and all these things will be given to you " (Matthew 6:33). This is what Paul meant when he said, "Having done everything . . . stand firm" (Ephesians 6:13). And this is what we meant when we inscribed on our coins "In God We Trust."

There is a hymn I hear every now and then. The chorus lingers with me a long time each time I hear it. It goes like this:

> Because I know he holds the future,
> And life is worth the living—just because he lives.
> ("Because He Lives," lyrics by Gloria and William J. Gaither, *United Methodist Hymnal*, #364)

So the point is clear. Reach out and wrap your arms around trust in God.

# CHAPTER FOUR

## Reach Out and Wrap Your Arms around Jesus and His Message

SCRIPTURE: MARK 14:43-50

Some years ago a young lawyer called me one morning to ask a favor. He wanted me to visit one of his clients who was at that moment behind bars, awaiting trial for armed robbery. When the lawyer said the prisoner's name, I recognized it immediately. There had been quite a bit of discussion and information about him in the newspapers and on television. He was from somewhere out west and had been painted by the media to be mean, wicked, ruthless, evil, unfeeling, and uncaring. He looked the part. His complexion was ruddy and rough and weather-beaten. His eyes were bleary. He had this cold, glassy-eyed stare, probably produced from too many drugs and too much alcohol. His arms were covered with cheap-looking tattoos, and his hair looked like a disheveled mass of dried straw. He was a tough looking character. He would have scared the wits out of Hannibal Lecter!

Even though he was handcuffed, I must confess that I felt a little uneasy as I was locked in his prison cell with him. I can remember as if it were yesterday: the sound of that cell door slamming shut and being locked and the jailor walking away and leaving me alone—all alone—with this hardened criminal.

I introduced myself and told him that his lawyer had sent me. He just glared at me with a fierce stare. There was a moment of awkward silence, which lasted only a few seconds, but it seemed like an eternity. Not really knowing what to say to this man or how I might help him in any way, I simply blurted out: "Why don't you tell me your story?" And he did. He started slowly, but soon the words were flowing easily as the truth of his story came out.

His father had beaten him unmercifully when he was a little boy. He had lots of scars to show for it. When he was eight years old, his father had deserted the family. His mother from that point on began to entertain a succession of men in their home. When he was about ten, his mother taught him how to steal and encouraged him to take anything he could get his hands on.

Later, as he entered his teen years, his mother turned him against every symbol of authority and responsibility. She taught him to hate the school, the church, and the law. When he was fourteen, his father returned home briefly and, in an alcoholic rage, almost killed both mother and child. He and his mother were taken to a charity hospital. When he was well enough, he slipped out of the hospital and ran away. To survive he did the only thing he knew how to do—rob and steal.

On and on he went with the tragic details of his story. As I listened to him, I had a strange mixture of feelings. I didn't feel so afraid of him anymore. I felt sorry for him. He had committed a long series of serious crimes in several states over many years, and he needed to be in prison. I knew that and he knew that. The community needed to be protected from him. And he told me that day that he wanted to be there! He had come to realize that he really needed and craved some sort of strong supervision.

Here was a man who, because of his traumatic early years, was now consumed with anger, was now a menace to himself and to his community, and was now unable to recall a single moment of any tenderness at all in his life. Here was a man who actually wanted to spend the rest of his years in prison. That's what he wanted to talk to me about. He wanted to tell a minister his story.

He wanted to tell a minister about this decision he had made to ask to be put behind bars for life. It was his way of trying to say, "I'm sorry." It was his way of trying to rectify and redeem a horrible situation.

As I listened to him, I made an important discovery that day, namely this: that everybody has a story to tell, and when you hear that story you will feel different toward them.

Shortly after that experience, I saw a movie about the arrest, trial, and crucifixion of Jesus. It was a bit overdone for my taste, but I remember how dramatically the character of Judas was portrayed. He was the heavy. From the very first moment, you knew beyond a shadow of a doubt that he was the bad guy. When he betrayed Jesus later in the movie, you expected it. And when he took his own life, you were easily convinced that it was an appropriate and fitting end for this evil character. But then, as with that man in the jail cell, I found myself wondering about Judas. I yearned to ask him, "Judas, what is your story? Judas, what is the real truth of your story?"

We are often reluctant to ask that question, aren't we? We much prefer that people come to us, not with a story, but in simple caricature. We want to know whether a person is a good guy or a bad guy. Does he wear a white hat or a black hat? And we are uncomfortable when someone says, "Well, it's not all that simple."

Have you heard about the man who was looking for a one-handed lawyer? "A one-handed lawyer?" asked his friend, "How come?" The reply was brusque: "I am looking for an attorney who won't say, 'On the one hand this, but on the other hand, that!' I want a one-handed lawyer."

I suppose we all want that: simple explanations to complex problems; a world where no one is just "so-so" but where everyone is either good or bad. Some of the early writers were like that with Judas. They probably didn't tell his story. They told their story about him, and they made of him a simplistic caricature—a bad guy! They painted him as a dramatically evil and wicked man, and history has dealt with him even more harshly, to the point that today no name carries such shame as that of Judas Iscariot. There is no feeling of sympathy toward him at all, almost to the point that we wonder if perhaps history has made him the scapegoat for the terrible things that happened to Jesus as he was arrested, tried, and crucified.

But I keep wondering, what is Judas's story? What is the real truth of Judas's story? Why did he betray his Master? Over the years, many answers have emerged. Let's brainstorm about them and see how many we can list.

Why did Judas betray Jesus? Did he do it for money?

Some have suggested that, saying Judas was undone by his greed and his love for money. But that really doesn't carry much weight because Judas could have struck a better bargain than that if his interest had been money. And remember also that almost immediately after Jesus was arrested, Judas threw the money back at them and then took his own life. Some say he did it for the money, but I don't think it can be that simple.

Was Judas a spy? Some have said that. They think he was planted among the disciples by the authorities of the day, placed there from the beginning to betray Jesus at just the right time. I don't know how you feel about this cloak-and-dagger idea, but again to me it seems too simple an explanation, more of a caricature idea than a real story.

Was it predestined that Judas should be the traitor? Was it predetermined that Judas would be the one to betray his Master? Some have said the answer is here. "It was written in the cards. It was all part of the plan." How do you feel about that? Do you agree with that? And if you do, then how do you balance that with God's grace and with God's gift of freedom of choice? Did Judas have a choice? Or was he predestined to betray? What do you think?

Still others say it was a political strategy on Judas's part. Maybe Judas was simply trying to force the issue, to bring the showdown, to make Jesus get on with it, to make Jesus act, to make Jesus go ahead and bring the kingdom with power. Judas might have reasoned, "I'll call his hand. I'll set it up. I'll put him in a position where he has no choice but to react with force, and more, to establish his kingdom. And when it's all over and done, he will thank me for it!"

What do you think? Do you think this was what was going on in the mind of Judas? Many bright scholars have believed this to be the case. But still others think that Judas just got scared and acted out of fear. The tides were turning against them. There was a groundswell of opposition, and these opponents were formidable. "Why did Jesus have to cause such a stir in the Temple? When he overturned the moneychangers' tables, and cleansed the Temple, he stepped on some mighty big toes," Judas may have thought. "They are really out to get him now and I could go down with him—'guilt by association,' they call it." Maybe Judas got scared and sold out simply to save his own skin.

Or maybe he just misunderstood Jesus and missed the whole point of who Jesus was and what he was trying to do. I rather suspect that we often do that too. We betray Jesus because we miss the whole point of who Jesus was and what he was trying to do. Let me show you what I mean.

## Judas Missed the Message

And sometimes so do we. On December 17, 1903, Orville and Wilbur Wright kept their hand-built airplane up in the air for fifty-nine seconds. It was an incredible accomplishment. Then they sent a telegram to their sister in Dayton, Ohio, which read:

> FIRST SUSTAINED FLIGHT TODAY 59 SECONDS. HOPE TO BE HOME FOR CHRISTMAS.

The excited sister took the incredible news to the local newspaper editor. The next morning to her shock and dismay, the headline read in bold letters:

> POPULAR LOCAL BICYCLE MERCHANTS TO BE HOME FOR HOLIDAYS

Incredible news—one of the biggest news stories in all of history—and it passed Dayton by that day because the editor had missed the message. How often that happens. We miss the message.

Jesus came preaching love, not force; forgiveness, not vengeance; mercy, not cruelty; kindness, not hatred—and we, like Judas, are still missing his message. We still believe in power and force. We still have too much vengeance and hostility in our lives. And we excuse ourselves by saying, "He didn't really mean it." But he showed us he meant it on the cross! So if we don't want to be a traitor to Christ, then we dare not—we must not—miss his message of love. Judas heard Jesus when he spoke of the Kingdom and the power and the glory. He evidently was not listening as carefully when Jesus said the road to the kingdom of God is by way of a cross. He missed the message, and sometimes so do we.

## Judas Missed the Mandate

And sometimes so do we. Of course the word *mandate* means *command*. The mandate of Jesus was to follow him. The command of Jesus was to trust, to be obedient, to be faithful. This was where Judas slipped up, perhaps. Maybe he was trying to ensure his success. Maybe Judas was trying to make Jesus do it his way. He tried to use Jesus. He tried to manipulate Jesus. Judas tried to play God and make it all come out his way.

Don't we still do that? Don't we still try to manipulate and use God? Think of your prayer life. What do you say in your prayers? God do this. God do that. God bless me. God fix my problem. God give to me. God work this out for me just like this.

We are called to be faithful, not to be successful. We are called to serve God and to be obedient to God. We are called to do the best we know and to trust God to bring it out right. But Judas missed the message and he missed the mandate.

## Judas Missed His Moment

Sometimes so do we. Actually Judas missed his key moments, which could have changed his life. If he had seized any one of them, then today his name would be an honored one rather than one of shame.

The first came in the Upper Room. Jesus offered bread to Judas. That was a very significant moment. It was the symbol of forgiveness. By custom, to dip a morsel of bread or meat into the dish and hand it to someone at the table was a token of deep personal friendship. Jesus was offering to Judas his love, his friendship, reconciliation, a way out of the deception, and forgiveness. In effect, Jesus was saying, "Judas, I know, and I still love you. It's not too late. You don't have to go through with this." The crowning blow was that even as Jesus offered this symbol of love and friendship, Judas made his final resolve to betray him. Jesus saw it in his eyes. "Do quickly what you are going to do" (John 13:27).

He could have been forgiven! All the disciples ran out, and they were all forgiven! Judas could have been forgiven too. He could have made a comeback. The big difference between Simon Peter and Judas is here. Peter failed too, but he recovered. He bounced back, but Judas thought his failure was final and he took his own life.

The unseized moments of life are the stuff tragedy is made of, the unseized moment of helping someone in need, of listening, of caring, of expressing appreciation, of giving or accepting forgiveness, of commitment.

Judas missed his moment and sometimes so do we.

A noted and respected theologian once visited Calcutta with Mother Teresa. He said they both saw the pain, poverty, and suffering. They both saw the great need there to help people. The theologian later lamented the fact that Mother Teresa saw the need and stayed to help while he went home and did nothing.

In life's great moments, what do you do? Judas missed the message, the mandate, and the moment, and that was his undoing. It could be our undoing too. Because, you see, while it's OK to grapple with this question, "Why did Judas betray?" the real question for us now is "Why do we?" And another crucial question for us right now is this: are we ready to reach out and wrap our arms around the message, the mandate, and the moment?

# CHAPTER FIVE

## Reach Out and Wrap Your Arms around a Sense of Purpose, Trust, and Love

SCRIPTURE: PHILIPPIANS 4:8-9

Have you heard the story about the two young men who broke into a department store in a big city one night? They were in the store for an hour or so, did what they came to do, and made their escape unnoticed. But here is where the story becomes intriguing.

The young men were not robbers. They didn't steal anything. They didn't remove a single item from the store. No—as a joke, these pranksters just changed the price tags on the merchandise! They changed the values! They repriced most everything in the store.

They took a $5 price tag off of a paperback book and

put it on a television set. They took the $400 price tag off the TV and put it on a necktie. They took the $350 price tag off a camera and put it on some $10 earmuffs, and they put the $10 earmuffs' sticker on a diamond necklace.

Now, what's really amazing about this story is what happened the next morning. The store opened as usual. The employees came to work as usual. Customers began to shop as usual. The department store functioned as usual all morning before anybody noticed that something was different. Some folks got some unbelievable buys. Others got ripped off. This all went on for over four hours before anyone realized that the price tags had been switched—the values had been changed.

This is a great parable for us today because all around us in our modern society, people are trying to do that to us. They are trying to change the price tags—switch the stickers—confuse and distort our values. They want to peddle the most valuable things for pennies and sell the cheapest things for millions.

For example, we pay millions to those who entertain and thrill us and pennies to those who teach us. There is something wrong with that picture! We adorn the body and degrade the soul. We pamper the skin and pollute the heart. People go on national television and joke about their numerous marriage failures. They openly and proudly tell of their use of drugs and alcohol, and—are you ready for this?—the audience laughs and applauds.

Who changed the price tags? Who switched our values? Who mixed up our priorities? Why does our society today sneer at time-honored values like the Ten Commandments, and instead applaud senseless, selfish, sordid standards of behavior like those we see on reality TV shows where the person who can lie and scheme and cheat and connive and deceive best is rewarded with a million-dollar prize?

Or look at what has happened in the world of comedy. The great comedians like Jack Benny, Carol Burnett, Bob Hope, Red Skelton, Lucille Ball, Bill Cosby, and Dick Van Dyke all made themselves the butt of their own jokes. They made fun of themselves. They laughed at themselves. We related to that and saw ourselves in them and their foibles, and we had a good healthy laugh at ourselves along with them. Sadly, so many of today's comedians do just the opposite: they make fun of other people, they trash other people, and if we don't laugh enough at that, they resort to obscenities and vulgarities.

Who changed the price tags? Who messed up our values? Who broke into the store and switched the stickers so that cheap thrills are going for top dollar and the value of human beings is at a distressing, disturbing low? What happened to respect and courtesy and graciousness and honesty and integrity and goodness and morality? And how do we turn it around? How do we make a difference? How do we remember and give energy to the things in life that really matter?

As always, the answer is in the Bible. We have the solution in our hands. We have had it all along. The Apostle Paul talked about this in Philippians 4. He tells us there what the real values are. Notice that Paul does not tell us to give our energy to whatever is false and deceitful and sordid and hateful and arrogant. He doesn't tell us to count those things as valuable. No! He saw just the reverse. He said, "whatever is true, whatever is honorable, whatever is just, whatever is pure, whatever is pleasing, whatever is commendable, if there is any excellence and if there is anything worthy of praise, think about these things. Keep on doing the things that you have learned and received and heard and seen in me, and the God of peace will be with you" (vv. 8-9).

And then Paul concludes this section of the letter with one of the greatest verses in all of the Bible, Philippians 4:13, one of the first verses of scripture many of us memorized when we were younger, "I can do all things through [Christ] who strengthens me." William Barclay translated it like this: "I can do all things through Christ who infuses his strength into me."

I also like the way one of my seminary professors paraphrased this verse. He put it like this: "Bring it on . . . I am ready for anything for Christ is within me." In other words, Paul is saying, "I'm not going to decay or degenerate spiritually. My faith is not going to break down or decompose or fall apart or lose focus, because I have the energy of Christ within me. I have the activity, the warmth, the life, and the spirit of Christ within me. That's what keeps me going. That's what keeps my faith alive and well and strong and focused on what's really valuable in life. It's true for us, too, isn't it? The only way we can keep spiritually alive and well and strong is to have the energy of Christ within us.

But what is that energy? What was it that energized Jesus Christ? What were his priorities? What was it that kept him going? What gave him strength and courage and confidence and poise? Many things, I'm sure, but let me for now suggest just a few. Maybe we can find some keys to zestful and abundant life somewhere between the lines.

## First of All, a Sacred Sense of Purpose

Jesus Christ placed high value on that—and we can, too. There's nothing more valuable or empowering than that—a sense of purpose, a sense of meaning, a sense of mission.

His purpose was spelled out clearly in the Gospel of

John: "For God so loved the world that he gave his only Son, so that everyone who believes in him may not perish but may have eternal life. Indeed, God did not send the Son into the world to condemn the world, but in order that the world might be saved through him" (3:16-17).

He came to redeem the world, to deliver and save people. He came to show us what God is like and what God wants us to be like. That was his mission and that was the power that energized him—the power of his great purpose to seek and save the lost and to redeem a sin-sick world.

That's what kept his eye on the ball. Let me illustrate it like this: Do you remember the story of Rapunzel? It's one of the fairy tales by the Brothers Grimm, the story of a beautiful girl named Rapunzel who lives with a wicked witch in a drab and dingy tower. The old witch is holding Rapunzel captive, and to keep her in her place, the wicked witch does two things: First, she removes all the mirrors from the tower so Rapunzel cannot see what she looks like. And then the old witch tells Rapunzel repeatedly that she is ugly. In fact, the witch says to her, "Rapunzel, you look just like me."

Since there are no mirrors in the tower, poor Rapunzel believes it. She can't see how beautiful she is, so she remains a prisoner in the tower, a prisoner to her own supposed ugliness. The witch believes that if Rapunzel is convinced of her ugliness, she will never try to escape from the tower. The witch has broken into the store and changed the price tags.

But then one bright day, a prince comes riding by on his white horse just as Rapunzel is leaning out of the tower for a breath of fresh air. Their eyes meet, and it is love at first sight. "Rapunzel! Rapunzel! Let down your hair," says the prince. She does just that. She lets her long flowing hair hang down from the balcony, and the prince climbs up into the tower.

But now look what happens. They gaze lovingly into each other's eyes, and Rapunzel sees in the glistening eyes of her prince a clear reflection of her own face. In the mirror of his eyes, Rapunzel sees for the first time that she is beautiful. And in that moment she is set free! Free from the witch! Free from the tower! Free from the past! Free from the feeling that she is ugly! Then the prince takes Rapunzel into his arms; they parachute onto his horse and ride happily off into the sunset.

It's a fairy tale to be sure, but there is a powerful message here for you and me. All of us are prisoners, all of us are captives, until Christ comes to set us free and we see in the reflection of his eyes that we are valuable. He comes saying to us, "You may have been living in a tower of ugliness, but you are beautiful to me; you are valuable to me; you are special to me." And as amazing as this may sound, he says, "You are worth dying for!" And he saves us. He delivers us from the ugly tower. He sets us free.

I like the way Lloyd C. Douglas expresses this in one of his novels. Jesus asks Zacchaeus why he wants to change his lifestyle. And Zacchaeus says that he wants to change, feels called to change, because he sees reflected in the Lord's eyes the person he could become, the person he was meant to be.

That was the purpose that energized and empowered Jesus Christ. He came to save and redeem people. That high value kept him focused. But that's not the end of the story, is it? We have to do our part. We have to accept his love. We have to accept his gift of salvation. And then when we do, we become a part of his purpose. We pass it on to others.

Writing to the Corinthians, Paul put it like this: "in Christ God was reconciling the world to himself, not counting their trespasses against them, and entrusting the message of reconciliation to us. So we are ambassadors for Christ, since God is making his appeal through us" (2 Corinthians 5:19-20).

Let me ask you something. Be honest now. When people look into your eyes, what do they see? Do they see acceptance or rejection; warmth or coldness; concern or indifference; love or prejudice? Can people see reflected in your eyes the Spirit of Christ? That is our purpose, to reflect the redemptive spirit of Jesus Christ. What an awesome task! And yet that's our purpose, to be God's agents of love and reconciliation, and that purpose will energize you. If you take that seriously and commit your life to it, it will keep your faith alive and well and strong. That's the first thing—Christ valued his sacred sense of purpose.

## Second, a Sacred Sense of Trust

Christ placed high value on that, and so can we. Jesus totally trusted the Father. "Thy will be done" was the theme of his life.

The noted theologian Søren Kierkegaard once told a parable about a certain rich man who bought a team of outstanding horses. But the rich man's coachman was inept and undisciplined and before long, you could hardly recognize the once proud horses. They were dull and drowsy, their pace was inconsistent, and their stamina gone. They developed strange quirks and bad habits. In frustration, the rich man called for help from the king's coachman, who knew horses very well. The king's coachman worked with the horses just a short period of time and when they became familiar with his voice, they became totally responsive to his commands. They held their heads high, their eyes were bright, and their pace became once again exquisitely beautiful. The potential was there all along. It all depended on whose voice they heard directing their lives.

Jesus was empowered and encouraged by that kind of trust in the Father. He heard God's voice, followed God's lead, and did God's will. There is great strength in knowing you can trust the Father to always be with you to guide you and watch over you and see you through; knowing that nothing—not even death—can separate you from God's love.

Do you trust God like that? Do you know the incredible power and poise that comes from trusting God like that? Victor Hugo once wrote a poem about a small bird resting on a tree branch that is about to break. Hugo ends the poem with these lines:

> She feels the branch tremble; yet gaily she sings,
> What is it to her? She has wings, she has wings.

Trust in God gives us wings! Christ placed high value, first, on a sense of purpose and, second, on a sense of trust.

### Third and Finally, a Sacred Sense of Love

Jesus Christ placed high value on that, and so can we. Years ago, a minister friend of mine served as a visiting lecturer. He said many great things in his lectures that challenged and inspired us, but what I remember most vividly was that last night when he told about buying a scarf for his daughter.

He was attending a ministry conference in the Far East when he saw this beautiful silk scarf. He bought it and brought it home as a gift for his daughter. She loved it, and he said he was amazed by what all she could do with that silk scarf. One day she would tie it around her neck. Another day she would wrap it around her waist. And some days she would drape it gracefully over her shoulder. And whatever she might be wearing, that scarf would make it even more attractive! Then my friend said *love* is like that. Wrap *love* around anything and it will enhance it. Wrap *love* around anything and it will make it more beautiful!

Jesus believed that with all of his heart. He practiced that daily, and it gave him great power. He wrapped love-energy around everything he did, and so should we.

The lesson of spiritual values is clear: if we want to keep our faith from decaying and breaking down, if we want to keep our faith alive and well and strong, then we need to receive from the Living Christ a sacred sense of purpose, of trust, and of love.

# CHAPTER SIX

## Reach Out and Wrap Your Arms around the Hunger for Righteousness

SCRIPTURE: MATTHEW 5:1-12

Many years ago, I had the special privilege of helping a young couple adopt a baby. They were originally from the Philippines, and they were thrilled beyond belief when, through Volunteers of America, we were able rather quickly to find them a two-month-old baby boy. And the very next Sunday morning in church, I had the privilege of baptizing him.

Not many weeks later, we entered the Christmas season, and on Christmas Eve, the proud new father called me to thank me again for helping them adopt his son. It was then that he said, "We now owe you a great debt of gratitude which must be repaid." "Oh no, no," I gently protested. "You don't owe me a thing. It was a joy for me to help you get your son. That is reward enough and then some." Then in a fashion typical of their courteous culture he said, "But our family has a Christmas gift for your family, and we would be dishonored if you did not accept it." "Oh, a Christmas gift! That's wonderful!" I responded. And then he said, "We have a dog for you!"

At that moment my heart sank. A dog? But that gift turned out to be one of the greatest Christmas gifts we ever received. That little Maltese dog quickly captured our hearts and became a very important member of our family. We named him Datu, which means "prince" in the Filipino language, a fitting name because, in princely fashion, he ruled over our household for almost seventeen years. He only weighed five pounds, and most of that was fluffy white hair, but he was a real heavyweight champion when it came to love, affection, and companionship.

Now, there were many fascinating things I could tell you about Datu, but the most remarkable was this incredible passion he had for his daily walk. He loved to go for a walk. If you would just take a step toward the door or act like you were going to pick up his leash, he would go into the most inspiring routine. His ears would perk up. His eyes would light up. His tail would wag. He would run and jump and celebrate. He would do back flips and cartwheels. He would cheer and applaud and he would yodel. Well, not quite all of that, but you get the picture.

The point is, he lived for that walk. He had a passion for his walk. He loved it. And there was absolutely no question about the intensity of that love. He became so excited and so animated that you could hardly keep him still long enough to get his leash on him.

Now when I saw his amazing joy, excitement, anticipation, and enthusiasm, I sometimes found myself thinking that everybody in the world should love *something* as much as Datu loved his walk.

Let me ask you something. Be honest, do you love anything like that? That much? With that kind of passion and commitment? Is there anything in your life right now that you can think of that inspires you, excites you, fills you, thrills you, stirs you, and motivates you like that? Do you know what Jesus said about this? A rather amazing thing—he said we should be that passionate, that enthusiastic, that fired-up in our pursuit of goodness and righteousness. Now, that's something to think about, isn't it?

Here's how our Lord put it in the fourth Beatitude: "Blessed are those who hunger and thirst for righteousness, for they will be filled." (Matthew 5:6). In other words, "Oh, how happy are those who strive for righteousness! Oh, how fulfilled are those who work for justice! Oh, how close to God are those who long for goodness! Oh, how near to the heart of God are those who crave godliness!" How is it with you right now? Do you want goodness as much as a starving man wants food? Do you want righteousness as much as someone stranded in the desert wants water? Or have you been looking for life and love and happiness in all the wrong places?

Some years ago, I was serving a church in West Tennessee when one of our young people, a fifteen-year-old boy, got stressed out by problems at school and ran away from home. For four days and nights, we looked for him, but no luck. Finally, on the fifth morning, word came that a policeman had found him. He was cold, scared, and hungry, but otherwise all right. The policeman would have him back home in thirty minutes or so. I went over to be with the family for his homecoming. When the policeman brought him in there were anxious hugs, tears, and apologies, and huge sighs of relief. Then we all went into the kitchen where his mother had fixed breakfast. As we walked in, that teenage boy, who had not eaten for four days, rushed to the table and never once thought to bother with the silverware. With both hands, he scooped up the scrambled eggs and grits and began to devour that food like a famished animal. I had never in my life seen anybody that starved for food.

Think about that—have you ever been that hungry for righteousness?

Jesus said, "Blessed are those [close to God] who hunger and thirst for righteousness." This Beatitude is really asking us a poignant question. In effect, it asks, "How much do you want goodness?" Do you want it as much as a starving person wants food or a thirsty person wants water or a drowning person wants air? Now of course, the key word here is *righteousness*. What on earth does that word mean? Well, as always, the Scriptures help us. In the Bible, the word *righteousness* is used in three different ways. Let's take a look at these together. Hopefully, we may find ourselves, or someone we know, somewhere between the lines.

## First, in the Scriptures, the Word *Righteousness* Means Personal Goodness

A few years ago at Annual Conference, the bishop asked the new young ministers who stood before him that haunting question that ministers are asked before they are ordained: "Are you going on to perfection?" Then quickly the bishop added, "If not, where are you going?"

In a sense that's what this fourth Beatitude says to us: Are you moving toward personal goodness? Are you trying to do better? Are you heading toward a deeper Christian commitment to morality? *If not, where are you going?*

All of us have seen hitchhikers who stand along the highways holding up signs that indicate where they would like to go, signs that reveal their hoped-for destination. Some are very specific, like Dallas, New Orleans, Denver, or Little Rock. Others are less exact: Florida, Michigan, or Tennessee. Still others are even more general: North, East, South, or West on I-10.

A friend of mine told me he saw a young man hitchhiking, one Christmas season not long ago, in Southern California, standing by the highway and holding up a sign which read, "Anywhere." Wouldn't you like to know the rest of that story? But the truth is that many people go through life like that. They will go anywhere life takes them. Wherever the fads of life, the moods of life, the waves of life take them they will go, just swept along with no sense of personal direction.

But here in the fourth Beatitude, Jesus reminds us that we need to stop drifting and start going in the direction of goodness in our personal lives, moving toward morality, pursuing character and ethics and cleanness.

I knew a minister out west who was called into the sanctuary early one morning. The custodian wanted him to see a strange offering that had been left on the altar. It was a pair of brown corduroy pants, a belt, a white T-shirt, a pair of tan suede boots, and a note. There were bloodstains on the shirt and the note. The note said, "Please listen to God." It was signed and there was a phone number. The minister dialed the number. A nineteen-year-old young man answered and told his story.

He had run away from home and had been wandering in a wasteland of drugs, drifting from one place to another, getting in all kinds of trouble and sordid behavior. The night before, he had hit bottom. There had been a struggle on the streets, a fight and an almost fatal beating. After making sure the victim of his uncontrolled assault was going to be all right in the emergency room of a nearby hospital, this young man came to the church, found an unlocked door, and went into the sanctuary.

He stayed there all night, crying, praying, and pondering. He asked God to forgive him and to show him the way to go. All at once the presence of God became very real. He knew God was there. He felt God's forgiveness. A wonderful peace came. He committed himself to follow Christ. He determined to make things right that he had messed up. He felt fresh and clean—like a new man. To symbolize his new life and new commitment, he had put on some new clothes he had with him in his bedroll and left the others as a kind of offering, giving God his old life. He walked out the door a new person, with a new vision, a new hope, a new life, and a new direction.

Why did he come to the church?

Why did he pray all night?

Why did he plead for forgiveness?

Why did he make that new commitment?

Why did he put on new clothes?

Because he was hungry for God, thirsty for goodness. When he came to his senses like the prodigal son, he wanted to come home to God. He realized that his soul was starving to death. He wanted to do better and be better.

Now, how about you and me? How much do we want the righteousness of personal goodness?

## Second, in the Scriptures, the Word *Righteousness* Also Means Social Justice

Many years ago a young lawyer made a trip to New Orleans and saw something happening there that broke his heart and turned his stomach: a slave auction. Slaves had been brought in by boat and they were being sold to the highest bidders. The sights and sounds of that moment were locked forever in the mind of that young lawyer. Slave children were crying. Women were screaming, and men were struggling helplessly against their shackles as families were torn apart, probably never to see each other again. Human beings were being treated like animals and sold into slavery. It was a cruel, sordid business, and that young lawyer watched the ugliness and the inhumanity of it all with tears in his eyes and he said, "This is wrong! Terribly wrong! And if I ever get a chance to strike a blow against this, I will do it with all my strength!"

Do you know who that young lawyer was? His name was Abraham Lincoln. In time his opportunity to right the wrong came, and he stood tall and struck the blow for justice.

A part of our calling as a church is to be the conscience of society and to stand tall for social justice. All through the Bible, we see it. Moses, Amos, Isaiah, Elijah, the Apostle Paul, and especially Jesus—all committed themselves not only to personal goodness but also to social justice.

How is it with you and me? How much do we want the righteousness of social justice?

## Finally, in the Scriptures the Word *Righteousness* Also Means Right Relationships

I read recently about a man who prayed, "O God, use me any way you desire, but especially in the advisory capacity." In the original Greek New Testament, the word for "righteousness" is *dikaiosuna*, and it literally means to "be set right with God and other people."

This is one of the major themes of the Bible. The

great command is to love God and people, and the best way to express our love for God is to show love for God's children. The prophets said it. So did Paul. And so did Jesus. But so often we forget this, don't we? Too often we ignore God, and too much we hurt each other.

Some years ago, a little eight-year-old girl was lost in the woods. It was winter—snowing, sleeting, and bitterly cold. Hundreds of people combed the forest, desperately searching for the little lost girl. Time was of the essence. They knew she couldn't survive long in this freezing weather. For hours and hours they looked and looked, but had no luck.

Finally, someone came up with the idea of having all the searchers join together and walk through the forest holding hands in a single line. They tried it, and in less than fifteen minutes they found her. But it was too late. She had died from cold and exposure. In the hush of that awful moment, someone said, "Why, oh why, didn't we join hands sooner?"

Sometimes when I see the troubles and conflicts in the world, I think about that: why, oh why, can't we join hands? This is what it means to hunger and thirst for righteousness—to strive energetically for personal goodness; to stand tall enthusiastically for social justice; and to join hands eagerly in right relationships with God and other people.

# CHAPTER SEVEN

## Reach Out and Wrap Your Arms around Spiritual Maturity

SCRIPTURE: LUKE 23:32-38

If I were to ask you to make a list of the most impressive qualities in the life and personality of Jesus, what would you write down? What would you jot down as Jesus' most striking characteristics? Of course, most people would top the list with love, followed quickly by commitment, courage, wisdom, humility, patience, mercy, and forbearance.

But I think there is another quality in the life of Jesus that—up to this point—we have not emphasized very much, but which probably should be ranked high on the list of his key attributes. I'm talking about his amazing maturity, his spiritual and emotional maturity. He was so young, only in his early thirties, but so mature. We see this vividly in our text from Luke 23. Listen again to these words.

The rulers scoffed at him. One of the criminals railed at him. The people stood by and gawked at him. The soldiers also mocked him. All together, they crucified him. And look how Jesus responded. He said, "Father, forgive them; for they do not know what they are doing" (Luke 23:34). That is the height of spiritual maturity.

They were ugly toward Jesus, but he refused to descend to their level. They were hateful toward him, but he refused to hate back. They were hostile toward him, but he remained unshaken. Jesus refused to take it personally. His integrity never wavered. He was mature enough to know that they were the ones with the problem, not him.

In 1963 a book came out and swept the country. It became very popular with psychologists and counselors all over America. It was written by Laura Huxley and was titled *You Are Not the Target*. In essence, the book said this: When people are upset and venting their anger toward you, when people are thoughtless or neglectful or difficult, just stop for a moment and take a breath. Realize that their irritability or hurtful behavior is not really aimed at you. It may feel like it is, but in all likelihood, you are not really the target. You just walked into their frustration (Laura Huxley, *You Are Not the Target* [New York: Farrar, Straus & Co., 1963], 37). You innocently walked into the fallout of somebody else's problem, and they projected the frustration out to you. This is a common experience in life.

Some years ago when our son Jeff was about five, we had some excitement in our neighborhood. Just down the street from our house, some puppies were born. A mother cocker spaniel gave birth to six beautiful cocker spaniel puppies, and all the children of the neighborhood were thrilled by the miracle of birth. Fifteen kids ran down to see the new puppies. Jeff was the last one to arrive. Fourteen children had already come to see the puppies, but when Jeff got there (number fifteen), the mother dog snapped at him. It absolutely broke his heart, and he ran home crying. He asked, "Dad, why did the mother dog snap at me? I wouldn't hurt the puppies. I love the puppies. I didn't mean any harm. Why did she bark at me?" And I said, "Jeff, don't take it personally. It wasn't you. It had nothing to do with you. The mother dog had a fourteen-kid tolerance and you were number fifteen. The mother dog was tired, and she took it out on you. You just walked by at the wrong time."

The point is clear: most of the time, when someone snaps at us, the person doing the snapping is really the one who has the problem. We are not the target. That's what Laura Huxley teaches us in her book. When her work was published, it was considered by many to be a significant psychological breakthrough—a new and helpful idea—and it is indeed helpful, but the truth is that Jesus taught us this in words and deeds a long time ago.

When someone is hateful toward you, that person is the one with the real problem, not you. So don't descend to their level. Take the high road. Help them with their problem if you can, but don't take it personally. Don't let their anger or insecurity or guilt or jealousy shake you, upset you, or defeat you. "When he was abused, he did not return abuse" (1 Peter 2:23). Jesus knew that they were the ones with the real problem, so he prayed for his persecutors. This magnanimous spirit is so important in life and in human relations. This Christian ability to not take it personally is one of the true marks of spiritual maturity.

Now, let me break this down a bit and bring it closer to home.

### First, When Someone Is Hostile with You, Don't Take It Personally

Some years ago, I served a church in West Tennessee. One Sunday morning, I went to the sanctuary early to be sure everything was ready for the worship service.

We were going to baptize a baby that morning, and I wanted to be sure there was water in the baptismal font. (Ministers have this occupational fear of reaching for the baptismal bowl and finding it dry as a bone.) It was a beautiful summer morning, and I was feeling good and whistling happily. As I walked over to the baptismal font, there was a man standing alone there at the altar. It was before 8:00 a.m. and no one else was around.

"Good morning, Bob," I said cheerily. Suddenly, Bob turned on me and in West Tennessee language he "cleaned my plow." He was angry and began to vent his wrath vociferously. He was complaining about "inefficiency in our society," how everything in our world—including the church—was being mismanaged. He was hot and hostile, and this was all seemingly prompted by the water in the baptismal font. "This water is dirty," he said. "Somebody should have cared for this. It's inexcusable!"

Actually, the water did look murky, but there was a good reason: only a few days before, a grandmother who had just returned from a tour of the Holy Land had added some water from the Jordan River for the baptism of her grandson. But Bob didn't want explanations. He was upset and he didn't want to be reasonable at that moment. On and on he went, red-faced and furious, spewing his hostility in my direction.

As I listened, I had two thoughts. First, I thought, "I've got a problem. Lord, please help me!" But then as I looked at Bob and listened as he went on and on, I suddenly realized something: "Hey! He's the one with the problem, not me. He's the one who is upset and red-faced and hot under the collar. I was happy when I walked in here. He's the one with the problem." So, silently, I prayed for him.

When he wound down, I reached over and touched his shoulder and I said: "Bob, I am so sorry that we have upset you. We love you, and we would never let you down on purpose. I'm glad that you love the church so much and that you want us to do everything right. Thanks for calling this to our attention. I'll bring it up in staff meeting in the morning. We'll try our best to do better."

Suddenly, he began to cry and apologize. We talked a bit longer, and then I changed the baptismal water and ran over to the chapel for the early communion service. After communion, as I came out of the chapel, someone was waiting for me. It was Bob's wife. She said, "Jim, I was in the narthex this morning, and I overheard how Bob talked to you. I wanted to tell you I'm sorry. He didn't mean that. He loves you. He loves this church." And then she said this: "You just walked into the middle of his hangover." The light bulb turned on.

Bob had had a rough Saturday night and on that Sunday morning, he was hurting physically and spiritually. He had a huge headache—accompanied by a sizeable guilt trip—and I had walked into his pain.

Now, here's the point. I could have thought, "Bob is a mean, cruel, heartless, and hostile man," but, he's not! He was just having a bad day, and I walked by at the wrong time. That is so often the case when someone is hostile with us. They have a problem that often we don't know about and can't see, and in their frustration they lash out at whoever walks by. When someone is hostile with you, remember that the one doing the snapping is the one with the real problem, and we have strolled into the fallout of someone else's problem and pain.

They were hostile with Jesus, and he prayed for them. They were hostile with Jesus, and he forgave them. They were hostile with Jesus, and he kept on loving them because Jesus knew that they were the ones with the real problem, not him! That bigness of spirit is a dramatic mark of Christian maturity.

## Second, When Someone Rejects You, Don't Take It Personally

It's hard not to take it personally when someone rejects you, but most of the time you are not the one with the problem.

Some years ago, I was serving a church in Central Ohio. One Monday morning, I came into the church office and found a man speaking harshly to one of our young secretaries. He was furious, shaking his finger in her face, raking her over the coals. I walked up just in time to hear him say, "I will never set foot in this church again!" Trying to help out—and rescue the young secretary, who was now in tears—I invited the man into my office, whereupon he turned on me.

He was upset about a letter he had received from the church that morning. The letter announced the formation of an important new committee. He had been put on the committee, no one had asked him ahead of time, and he was irate. As I listened to him vent his frustrations, I had two thoughts:

First, I knew he was overreacting. It was an important committee, but the truth is that if he never made a single meeting, it would not be the end of the world. I knew there must be something deeper eating at him.

Second, I also knew that he was acting out of character. I had known him for some time. He was basically a kind and gentle man who loved the church intensely. Something was wrong in his life, but I didn't know what it was.

I apologized. I told him that I thought someone had checked with him in advance, but evidently we had let it fall through the cracks and we were sorry. I told him that, of course, he didn't have to serve on the committee, but that he was the one person in the whole church that the chairman had handpicked for this significant job. Again, I apologized and said I hoped he could find it in his heart to forgive us.

He began to cry. Then he said, "Jim, I'm so sorry. You know this is not like me. I don't know why I let it upset me so. I'm the one who should ask for forgiveness." We talked some more and had a prayer together. Then he went out to make peace with that young secretary. I was puzzled. I couldn't figure out why the letter from the church had angered him so.

An hour or so later, I got my answer. His twenty-three-year-old daughter showed up at my office in tears. "Jim," she said, "I have to talk to somebody. Last Friday night my husband deserted me. He is not coming back and I don't know what I'm going to do. I have two babies and no job. I've cried all weekend. I haven't told anybody yet. I haven't even told Mother." Then she said, "I did call Daddy to tell him this morning."

The light bulb came on. Her dad had gone to work that morning and received this call from his daughter saying her husband had left her. He hung up the phone and—angry, worried, frustrated—he reached over for his mail. There on the top was this letter from the church, and we caught the whole load of his frustration.

Here's the point. We could have thought, "That is a mean, harsh man who hates and rejects the church," but he's not! We just walked by when he was hurting. We walked into his pain.

They rejected Jesus, but he didn't reject them. They rejected Jesus, but he didn't take it personally because he knew that they were the ones with the real problem, not him.

### Now, Finally, What Do We Do When Someone Lashes Out at Us?

As I see it, when someone lashes out at us, we have three possible choices:

First, there is the childish response, which is to run away and hide and cry because somebody is picking on us. Unless, of course, we find ourselves in a situation that is dangerous or physically harmful, leaving is not the answer.

Second, there is the adolescent response, which is to fight back, to strike back, or to get even. The problem here is that we descend to their level, so in most cases that is not the answer either.

Third, there is the mature adult response, which is to perform what I call the ministry of absorption, absorbing the hostilities but not taking them personally. This is the way of Christian strength. It's the ministry of trying to help people work through their problems, but not letting the spill-off of their anger or jealousy or insecurity or frustration shake us or upset us or defeat us.

"Turning the other cheek," "going the second mile," "loving our enemies," "praying for those who persecute us." Whatever you want to call it, it means recognizing that the person lashing out is really the one who has the problem.

They scoffed at him, railed at him, mocked him, crucified him, and Jesus said: "Father, forgive them, they know not what they do."

The poet Edwin Markham expressed it like this:

> He drew a circle that shut me out
> Heretic, rebel, a thing to flout.
> But love and I had the wit to win
> We drew a circle that took him in.
> (from "Outwitted," *The Shoes of Happiness, and Other Poems* [Garden City, N.Y.: Country Life Press, 1913])

So reach out and wrap your arms around spiritual maturity and, of course, the way you do that is to try every day, with the help of God, to become more like the Master.

# CHAPTER EIGHT

# Reach Out and Wrap Your Arms around the Spirit of Compassion

SCRIPTURE: LUKE 8:40-48

Some years ago, it was attributed to Ralph Waldo Emerson that he wrote these powerful words:

> To laugh often and much; to win the respect of intelligent people and the affection of children; to earn the appreciation of honest critics and endure the betrayal of false friends; to appreciate beauty; to find the best in others; to leave the world a bit better, whether by a healthy child, a garden patch or a redeemed social condition; to know even one life has breathed easier because you lived—that is to have succeeded.

I like that very much. It is a beautiful statement, but somehow I want to add one more ingredient to the mix—namely, compassion! The spirit of compassion, the touch of compassion—without that special Christian quality in our lives, our lives cannot be truly successful! We can be highly educated, we can rise to places of prominence in this world, we can accumulate lots of wealth, and we can even win numerous awards. However, even after we have done all those things, if we are not loving compassionate people, *our* lives are failures, empty shells, because we have missed the key component in life and God's most important lesson.

Loving compassion, Jesus called it, the most significant sign of discipleship. In John's Gospel, he said it like this: "I give you a new commandment, that you love one another. Just as I have loved you, you also should love one another. By this everyone will know that you are my disciples, if you have love for one another" (13:34-35). Jesus not only taught compassion but also lived it! As deftly and as quickly as a magnetic needle points to the North Star, even so the heart of Jesus immediately zeroed in on the neediest person in any crowd.

How quickly he noticed a rejected and lonely Zacchaeus up in that sycamore tree. How swiftly he sensed the intensity and urgency in the cry of blind Bartimaeus on the roadside. And in each case, Jesus reached out with compassion to give the help that was needed. Now, we see it again in this tender story in Luke 8. Remember the story with me.

Jesus is on his way to see a little girl who is critically ill, when suddenly he is interrupted. As Jesus is moving through a large enthusiastic crowd, a woman who has been hemorrhaging nonstop for twelve years discreetly slips up behind him and timidly touches the hem of his robe. Right then, the story tells us, her bleeding stops. She thinks she has gone unnoticed, so she drops back trying to lose herself in the huge crowd. But Jesus stops, turns around, and asks, "Who touched me?" His disciples are astonished and somewhat put out by his question. "Who touched you? What do you mean who touched you? The crowd is pressing in all around us, pushing and shoving. Everybody is touching everybody. What kind of question is that?"

But Jesus knows that it was a special touch. How perceptive he was! He begins to look around. The woman had not expected to be found out. But now she fearfully steps forward and tells Jesus that she has had this bleeding for so long and that she has tried everything—doctors, medicines, magic, wives' tales, superstitions—but to no avail, no improvement. In fact, she has only gotten worse. She tells Jesus that she has heard about him and his power to heal and that she felt that if she could just touch his clothing, she could be made well—and it worked! It worked! The bleeding has stopped. Jesus' heart goes out to her, and he speaks to her tenderly:

"Daughter, your faith has made you well; go in peace" (v. 48).

Now, in this fascinating story, we not only see the compassionate spirit of Jesus but also discover some of the key characteristics of compassion, special qualities that we, as followers of Jesus, need to cultivate in our lives. Let's take a look at some of these together.

### First, Compassion Is Sensitive

Compassion is aware, tuned in, responsive, and sensitive to the needs of others. Hundreds of people were pressing upon Jesus that day, thronging around him, pushing and touching him, yet out of that mass of humanity he was aware of one person, one need, one touch. How sensitive he was! To bring this closer to home, let me tell you a true story that happened to some friends of mine.

Paul and Ann had joined four other married couples on a weekend duck hunt in South Texas. As they prepared for the long drive home, Paul put his beloved hunting dogs in their travel kennels in the back of the station wagon. Ann was not feeling well, so she stretched out across the back seat to take a nap as Paul drove toward home. All went well until they stopped for gas in a small South Texas town. Paul then went to the back of the station wagon to check on the dogs. Just about then, Ann woke up with a headache and went into the service station office to take an aspirin. While she was there, Paul unwittingly jumped into the car and drove toward home! Ann came out just in time to see him pulling away. She ran after him, but he didn't see her.

She stood there thinking, "Well, he will miss me in a minute and come back." Fortunately, one of the other couples from the duck hunt drove by a little later and picked her up. She explained what had happened and then said, "Paul will miss me in a minute and turn back, so let's watch for him." *Two and a half hours later*, Paul got sleepy and reached back over the seat to wake Ann up to see if she felt like driving for a while. Imagine his surprise! Quickly, he figured out what had happened. He turned around hurriedly and headed back to find his wife. Shortly, he saw the other car, and Paul and Ann were reunited. However, Ann was not happy! Paul apologized. Profusely, he apologized. Eloquently, he apologized. Agonizingly, he apologized. Ann made no response. She just sat there smoldering. They rode along in silence. Finally, after some time she spoke: "I only have one thing to say: you never would have left your dogs!"

Eventually all was forgiven, but at that moment Ann did not think Paul had been very sensitive. She also thought he had his priorities mixed up. But let's not be too hard on Paul. We are all guilty. All of us have our moments like that when we neglect someone or ignore someone or even hurt someone. The disciples did that a lot. All through the Gospels, the disciples were doing or saying insensitive things. Remember how they tried to hold back the little children and how they squabbled over petty things? Here again in Luke 8 they get frustrated with Jesus when he stops to help this sick woman. Over and over, Jesus has to remind them (and us) to tune in to the needs of people, to be aware, to be sensitive. Compassion is sensitive to the needs of others.

## Second, Compassion Takes Advantage of Interruptions

This week, I skimmed through the Gospels and put together what I consider to be a very impressive list. Look at this listing and see if you can find the common thread that runs through these. Here it is:

- The Good Samaritan Parable
- The Greatest Commandment
- The Blessing of the Little Children
- The Healing of the Gerasene Demoniac
- The Healing of the Ten Lepers
- The Healing of the Paralytic

- The Healing of the Man Blind from Birth
- The Rich Young Ruler
- Zacchaeus
- Blind Bartimaeus
- Nicodemus
- The Cross and the Resurrection

What do these stories have in common? They are all special moments in the Scriptures, and they were all produced by *interruptions*! Jesus, with his compassionate heart, took advantage of these interruptions and redeemed them and used them to do good. We see it again here in Luke 8. Jesus *is* on his way to see the critically ill daughter of Jairus, when he heals this woman of her hemorrhage. This raises a poignant question that should haunt all of us: How many special moments have we missed? How many special moments with our children, our mates, our friends, our co-workers, or even with strangers, have we missed because we were too tired, too busy, or too preoccupied? Compassion is sensitive to the needs of others, and compassion takes advantage of interruptions.

## Third and Finally, Compassion Is Gracious

Notice how gracious Jesus is to the woman. He calls her "daughter," an obvious term of endearment. He doesn't fuss at her or criticize her or question her. He doesn't condemn her for being superstitious. He doesn't even give her a theology lesson. He just meets her where she is. He accepts her, encourages her, and heals her in a gracious way. And notice that he doesn't take the credit—he gives her faith the credit. "Your faith has made you well!" How gracious he was.

I have been in the ministry now for many, many years, and over the years I have noticed something that I think is very significant. The great Christians all possess this magnificent spirit of graciousness and humility.

Recently, while on a speaking engagement, I was at a dinner party in another state. The host was bragging loudly about how he had been active in a great church in that city for over thirty years and especially about how close he was to a series of truly outstanding ministers who had served that church during that span of time. But then when a certain man's name was mentioned he became livid. I cringed inside as he let loose with a harsh, hostile tirade against that other man. His criticism was hard, tough, cruel, unfair, vindictive—and was sprinkled with expletives. He finished by saying: "I'll never speak to him again as long as I live!"

I found myself wondering: What has he been hearing in church all these years? How could he go to church regularly for over thirty years and hear the gospel preached by those outstanding ministers Sunday after Sunday for all those years and still know nothing of graciousness, compassion, or forgiveness? I mean, how can we be exposed to the life and teachings and the spirit of Jesus and not realize the importance of love, mercy, and grace? Compassion is sensitive; it takes advantage of interruptions; it is gracious. Our Lord's bigness of spirit—our Lord's love—is a constant call and challenge to us to be compassionate, gracious people.

# CHAPTER NINE

## Reach Out and Wrap Your Arms around Your Christian Witness

SCRIPTURE: 2 CORINTHIANS 5:16-21

Some years ago, a book titled *The Bridge over the River Kwai* came off the presses and soon became a best-seller. Not only that, but the movie based upon it won several Academy Awards. In addition, the theme song of that movie, "The Colonel Bogey March," soared to the top of hit parades all over the country.

Later, another book was written about the River Kwai and I'd like to share that story with you. This book, Ernest Gordon's *Through the Valley of the Kwai*, is a true story of life as it was in the prisoner of war camps along the River Kwai during World War II, a spiritual adventure told by a man who lived it, a man who was himself a prisoner of war there for three and one-half years, a man who personally experienced the horrors of such an existence and lived to tell of it.

Ernest Gordon was a skeptic, a doubter, a non-believer, when he was first captured. Life in that prison camp was indescribably horrible. The prisoners of war were diseased, starved, tortured, and overworked. The guards violated every civilized code. They murdered prisoners openly by bayoneting, shooting, drowning, or decapitation. They murdered them subtly by working them beyond human endurance, starving them, torturing them, and denying them medical care. Needless to say, morale in the camp was very low. The prisoners felt defeated, afraid, and hopeless.

They turned to religion, but it was the wrong kind. Their religion was selfish: "Look, Lord, I'm in trouble here, I will speak well of you if you'll just get me out of this. Don't worry about the others, just help *me*." When the crutch of selfish religion didn't work for them, they threw it away.

Next, they tried the law of the jungle, survival of the fittest, every man for himself. They stole from each other; they cheated each other; they cursed and fought each other. The weak were trampled, the sick ignored, and the dead forgotten. Hate for some was the only motivation for living.

Then, they moved into despair and indifference.

They allowed cobras and other poisonous snakes to crawl right over them. They didn't care. Death called to them from every direction. It was in the air they breathed, it was the topic of every conversation. It was easier to die than to live.

But then, all of a sudden, everything changed. It turned completely around. Their despair gave way to hope, their hatred was turned into love, and their curses were replaced by prayers. Their complete indifference became radiant faith.

But how? What happened? What caused this miraculous transformation? Simply this: a new prisoner came into the camp. His name was Dusty Miller, and he came into that prison camp, into that horrible existence, as a Christian (I'm proud to say a Methodist Christian). And he just lived his faith.

He seemed to have the answer. Somehow Jesus Christ was in Dusty Miller. He radiated Christ and the Christian lifestyle. Every day he served God by serving his neighbors. He put others first. He shared his food and medicine. He cared for the sick and injured. Each night, even though he was exhausted too, he made his way through the camp checking on others, displaying the amazing quality of Christlike love. His spirit was contagious. Others began to act like him, and the Christian faith spread through the camp like wildfire.

The whole life of that camp was transformed. They helped one another. They cared for one another. They prayed for each other. They made artificial limbs for those who needed them. They made anesthetics from the plants of the jungle. They gave their lives for each other. And they started a university in the prison camp, a library, a drama society, a forty-piece orchestra, and they built a church in the jungle—all because one man shared his faith by living it.

You may be wondering what happened to Ernest Gordon and Dusty Miller. Well, Ernest Gordon survived and he wrote the book. He was called to the ministry through that experience in the Kwai Valley and became Dean of the Chapel at Princeton University.

What happened to Dusty Miller? The guards turned on him. They couldn't break him, so they hated him. They despised his goodness, and—unbelievably—they crucified him. Like his master, he died strung up to a tree, far from his home but so near to the heart of God.

This remarkable true story shows us dramatically what the Apostle Paul was talking about in 2 Corinthians when he said: "we are ambassadors for Christ, since God is making his appeal through us" (5:20). He has entrusted to us the message of reconciliation and wants us to pass it on to others. We are called to be God's representatives, God's witnesses, God's light in the world.

Dusty Miller understood that and he lived it. The question is, how is it with us? What about our influence? How well do we represent God? How can we effectively share our faith with others?

Let me suggest three basic answers: reverently, relevantly, and redemptively. Let's take a look at these "three R's" one at a time and see how we are doing as ambassadors for Christ.

## First, Reverently

The ambassador for Christ shares his or her faith with others reverently, that is, with reverence for God and with respect for others, with humility and kindness.

Each week, a number of church papers from all over the country come across my desk. One of them had in it an article announcing a workshop on evangelism, a workshop on personal witnessing. Nothing unusual about that. But what caught my eye was the theme of the workshop: "Can you share your faith without being obnoxious?"

In my lifetime, I have known some people who could benefit from that workshop. We have to be careful to not be arrogant or presumptuous or obnoxious when we try to share our faith with others.

Have you heard about the little boy who was told to come directly home from school, but every day arrived home late—sometimes ten, twenty, or thirty minutes late? His mother asked him about it. "Look, son, you get out of school the same time every day. Why can't you get home at the same time?" He answered, "It all depends on the cars." "What do cars have to do with it?" asked his mother. The youngster explained, "The safety patrol boy who takes us across the street makes us wait until some cars come along so he can stop them!"

We can get so caught up in our own self-importance, can't we? And sometimes folks do that as they try to share their faith with others. They forget about reverence for God and respect for others. Let me show you what I mean.

I knew a very bright ministerial student. He was sent to be the pastor of a small church out in the country, and he was offended. He felt that this small church was beneath him. He had studied Barth, Bultmann, Tillich, and Bonhoeffer. He had made straight A's in seminary so far. He had a working knowledge of Greek and Hebrew, and now they had sent him to this small rural church, and he was upset.

The Saturday morning before his first sermon an elderly church lay leader stopped by the parsonage. "Do you have your sermon ready, Pastor?" he asked. The minister answered, "The sermon is the least of my worries. I'm well-trained, and I won't need much preparation to preach to this uneducated congregation." The lay leader smiled, patted him on the shoulder, and said, "I'll be there, and I'll be rooting for you."

On Sunday morning, the young minister strode into the pulpit arrogantly, pompously, and—two minutes into his sermon—he went blank. He stood there mortified, unable to speak, unable to say anything. Finally, he lowered his head, stammered out an apology, and humbly walked out of the pulpit and out of the church. He sat down under a tree in the little cemetery next to the church. Head down, tears welling up in his eyes, he sat there in stunned silence.

Suddenly, the elderly lay leader sat down beside him. "It was horrible, wasn't it?" the young minister said. "Oh, it wasn't that bad," answered the old man. "I think you have a wonderful future in the ministry. You are bright, talented, committed, and well-educated. I've been around awhile and, if you'll let me, I would like to make just one suggestion. Every Sunday, if you could walk into the pulpit the way you just walked out of it, everything will work out fine."

Now, what was he talking about? Humility. Reverence. Reverence for God and respect for people. That's the first thing to remember when we start out to share our faith with other people—to do it reverently.

## Second, Relevantly

The ambassador for Christ shares his or her faith with others relevantly. The word *relevant* means "bearing upon or connected with the matter at hand." This means that we need to show people that the Christian faith can work for them now. It can touch their lives, change their lives, and save their lives. We are not just speaking high-sounding words into the air; we are sharing a Savior who can hear their cries, heal their hurts, calm their fears, and give meaning to their existence.

Remember the story about the fifth-grade Sunday school class learning a Bible memory verse. There were ten children in the class, eight girls and two boys. The verse was the King James Version of Romans 12:17 and 21, "Recompense to no man evil for evil... but overcome evil with good." The eight little girls got it immediately, followed pretty quickly by one of the boys. Nine of them had learned the verse and said it out loud. But the other boy couldn't say the word *recompense*. The other children began to laugh at him and tease him, especially his little buddy who was seated beside him elbowing him and calling him a dummy.

Finally, the little boy closed his eyes tightly and with every ounce of energy within him, he painstakingly blurted it out: "Recompense to no man evil for evil...but overcome evil with good!" Then without even stopping to catch his breath, he turned to his little buddy and said, "And as soon as I get you out of this church, I'm going to knock your block off," which was a complete contradiction of what he had supposedly just learned.

Don't misunderstand me. I'm not against memorizing Bible verses. I'm very much for that. I'm simply saying that it needs to be relevant. It needs to be appropriated to our lives. It's more than words—it's meaning: When we share our faith with others, we need to relate it to their lives. When we share our faith with others, we want to be very careful to do it reverently and relevantly.

### And Last, Redemptively

The ambassador for Christ shares his or her faith with others redemptively—that is, in a way that causes change to happen for the good.

Dr. Fred Craddock tells about a family out for a drive on a Sunday afternoon. All is going nicely when suddenly the two little children in the back seat begin to pound their father on the back.

> "Daddy, Daddy, stop the car! There's a kitten back there on the side of the road!"
>
> The father says, "So..."

"But, Daddy, if you don't [stop and pick it up] it will die."

"...We don't have room for another animal....No more animals....Be quiet, children...."

"We never thought our Daddy would be so mean and cruel as to let a little kitten die."

Finally, the mother turns to her husband and says, "Dear, you'll have to stop."

Of course, the father turns the car around, and they return to rescue the kitten, which upon closer inspection appears thin, starving, and infested with fleas. But when he reaches for the kitten, rather than being thankful, it lashes out and scratches him! Finally, after some maneuvering, he catches the kitten and brings it to the car, telling his children not to touch it—it's probably diseased! But the children hold the kitten and stroke it and talk to it and sing to it.

When they get home, the children feed the kitten, bathe the kitten, fix it a comfortable bed, and give it some toys to play with—and they hug it a lot. Weeks go by, and then one night, the father is sitting alone in the den reading the paper when something rubs against his leg and then jumps into his lap and curls up lovingly. It's the kitten. The father reaches down to tenderly stroke the cat. This time, the kitten does not hiss or scratch. Instead it purrs contentedly and snuggles down.

Wait a minute: Is this the same cat? In a way, no—it's not the scared and injured creature from before. This cat has been changed, redeemed. Now, what changed it? Love! That's what love can do. If you want to share your faith, that's how to do it (*Craddock Stories* [St. Louis: Chalice Press, 2001], 24–25).

Not long ago, God reached out to bless me. I looked at God's hand and guess what? It was covered with scratches: Such is the hand of love. How do we share our faith with others? Reverently, relevantly, and redemptively.

# CHAPTER TEN

## Reach Out and Wrap Your Arms around Your Christian Conscience

SCRIPTURE: ROMANS 7:18-25

When we talk about religion, eventually we get around to the question of morality, the question of ethics. Right or wrong, good or bad—how do we tell the difference?

Let's candidly admit it is not always easy to make the distinction. History documents this. For example, many of the people who put Jesus on the cross and the Apostle Paul in prison honestly thought they were doing the right thing. It's strangely and tragically true that some of the worst things that have ever happened in human history, people did conscientiously, honestly thinking they were doing what was right.

Remember the Crusades, the Inquisition, the Salem

witch hunts, to name just a few. Bloody wars, cruel persecutions, shameful prejudice, hateful discriminations, and brutal rituals—even human sacrifices. All have happened historically, performed by people in the name of "rightness."

In our own time, we have been jolted by Jonestown, the mass suicide of hundreds—913 found dead, and of that number 276 were children—and later by the events in Iran, where the Ayatollah Khomenei and the militant students held fifty Americans hostage for days and days in the name of religion.

Now, in recent days, we have the media blitz over scandals involving well-known religious leaders. It makes us wonder aloud and cringe within. We see it vividly in the political arena too, typified perhaps most dramatically by politicians who when questioned about personal morality say quizzically, "Why are you asking me that? It's irrelevant; my private behavior has nothing to do with my ability." Then they add, as if this justified it, "Besides, politicians have always done this sort of thing!"

The point is clear. We do get confused and perplexed in making ethical decisions. Right or wrong, good or bad, constructive or destructive, helpful or harmful—how do we tell the difference?

Most of us can identify with the little boy who

brought home a report card with terrible grades in conduct. His only explanation was, "But, Mom, conduct is my hardest subject." It is exactly so with us, isn't it? Again and again, we find it hard to know and to do what is right. Conduct is, indeed, our hardest subject.

Remember how the Apostle Paul put it in his letter to the Romans. Chapter 7 puts it graphically, "I do not understand my own actions. For I do not do what I want, but I do the very thing I hate. . . . I can will what is right, but I cannot do it. . . . Wretched man that I am!" (vv. 15-24).

Now, this is one passage of scripture that needs no explanation. We have all been there. We know what Paul means. How well we know from our own experience. Sometimes it is hard to determine the best action. Then sometimes, even when we think we know what is right, we still have trouble doing it.

What is the answer to the moral dilemma? How do we tell right from wrong? How do we make these hard ethical decisions? Some say to let your conscience be your guide. When you come to a fork in the ethical road, simply let your conscience be your guide. But the question is, "Can we?" Can we simply follow our consciences when faced with questions of right and wrong? What do you think? Can your conscience be your guide?

My answer is yes—and no! Yes, your conscience may

help you but also your conscience may be tricked or distorted or ignored or worn down. Let's look at this more closely by thinking together about three ideas.

## First, We All Have a Conscience

All sane, normal people have a sense of "oughtness" and conscience, which we use in varying ways and in varying degrees.

I heard a man joke one time that his conscience was "good as new, because it has never been used."

I heard another man joke that he had never developed a conscience because he considered it a liability. He said, "It never really kept me from doing anything anyway; it only kept me from enjoying it!"

All normal human beings feel the pangs of conscience. Most people have a sense of what is right and what is wrong, even though we don't always choose to do the right thing. Experts tell us that psychotic people have no sense of conscience, but the rest of us do.

Huckleberry Finn said that a conscience "takes up more room than all the rest of a person's insides" (Mark Twain, *The Adventures of Huckleberry Finn*, 1884 ed. [Nashville: American Renaissance Books, 2009], 155). We all have a conscience, and the only time that conscience becomes a problem for us is when it gets distorted or diseased.

Now, that brings us to point number two.

## Second, Our Conscience Can Be Tricked or Corrupted

Let me show you what I mean by listing here some distortions of conscience that I know about.

*First, There Is the Worn-Down Conscience*

Remember the old pinwheel illustration. The old-timers used to tell their children that a conscience is like a pinwheel in your head and that when you start to do something wrong, it spins and sticks and reminds you of your values. However, if it spins enough and rubs enough, it will wear down. It still spins, but it's worn down and doesn't stick anymore. Thus, those things once considered wrong or hurtful don't seem wrong anymore.

During World War II, an American soldier went with his buddies to a brothel in Paris. But his conscience touched him, so he waited outside. The second time, he went in to look around. The third time, he said, "I can't go! I can't. The first time I waited outside. The second time I went in just to look around. I know if I go back I will participate. I must not go again!" You see, that young soldier realized that we can wear down our consciences to the point where what once seemed wrong doesn't seem wrong anymore.

*Second, There Is the Rationalized Conscience*

This occurs when we trick our consciences with eloquent explanations. Remember in Tolstoy's *War and Peace* how the main character Pierre expresses it so graphically: "Yes, Lord, I have sinned, but I have several excellent excuses!"

Several years ago, I did a youth lecture series in a small town in West Tennessee. We were discussing ethics.

The young people said: "It's wrong to cheat, except in Latin." Their rationalization went like this: "The teacher is no good and unfair, and since she is not doing a good job, it's OK to cheat. Besides, everybody else does."

And those young people said, "It's wrong to gamble, except in our golf matches! It's only a quarter a hole," they said. "No one loses very much, and it makes the match more exciting."

That kind of rationalizing is dangerous. It can only lead to shaky ground when we rationalize our consciences.

*Third, There Is the Consequence Conscience*

A consequence conscience is another distorted conscience that only worries about getting caught. Let me show you what I mean.

A few years ago, I was going home one evening and I

was running late. Driving fast down the speedway that was a 25-mile-per-hour zone, I was going close to 40 when suddenly I saw, parked on a side road, a police car. My foot hit the brake, my heart jumped up in my mouth, and my conscience stirred powerfully within me. I waved to the policeman—and he waved back!

As I drove on heading home, constantly and nervously I kept glancing into the rear-view mirror to see if he was coming after me. That was the consequence conscience. I didn't feel bad about driving 40 miles per hour in a 25-mile-per-hour zone. What got to me was the fact that I almost got caught!

There is a big difference between those two. If the fear of the consequences is my only motivation, my only guide for doing right, then there is something wrong with me.

*Fourth Is the Childish Conscience*

Now, the problem here is that this is basically a negative approach to life, which leans heavily on the "Thou Shalt Nots." There is no involvement here with great social issues or adult loyalties or faith commitments, only the notion that some things are forbidden and, if you do them, you have to take the punishment.

There is much guilt and anxiety here, especially over having too much fun. The strange notion here is that

God is some sort of tyrant who watches us with a critical eye and says, "Now you have had so much fun, you must suffer so much punishment."

This was at least a part of the problem with the Pharisees. They had quite a conscience over ceremonial hand-washing and other minute details of the law but they omitted the more important matters of love, mercy, faith, justice, and compassion.

Worn-down conscience, rationalized conscience, consequence conscience, childish conscience—all are distortions. They are diseased and corrupted and, therefore, are not trustworthy.

That brings us to point number three.

## Third, We Can Cultivate a Christian Conscience

How do we do that? Let me illustrate it like this: Suppose I ask a group of people in your church this question: "How wide is the pulpit in your sanctuary?" Some might say 24 inches. Others might say 25 inches. Still others might say 27-3/4 inches. Now, these are all good guesses, but they can't all be correct. One of them is closer to the real truth than the others. So, how do we determine which one is right? How do we know which is correct and true? We have to get a measuring stick! We measure it with a measuring stick and then we can know which answer is right.

This is also true in matters of ethics and morality: Jesus Christ is our measuring stick! Jesus Christ is our model, our example, our blueprint. Here is the key to Christian conscience: to test everything, every decision, every action, by the measuring stick of Christ.

Helen Keller said something in her autobiography very interesting about her teacher. It is so powerful that it sounds almost as if she were talking about Christ. She was speaking about her teacher, Ann Sullivan, and she said these words:

> My teacher is so near to me that I scarcely think of myself apart from her. I feel that her being is inseparable from my own . . . and that the foot-steps of my life are in hers. All the best of me belongs to her! There is not a talent or an aspiration or a joy in me that has not been awakened by her loving touch!
> (*The Story of My Life* [Garden City, N.Y.: Country Life Press, 1904], 39)

That's the good news, isn't it? Christ is to us what Ann Sullivan was to Helen Keller, and yet much, much more. He is our teacher. He becomes our eyes, our ears, and our measuring stick. He is our conscience, and he is our Savior! The Apostle Paul put it powerfully like this: "Wretched man that I am! Who will rescue me from this body of death? Thanks be to God through Jesus Christ our Lord!" (Romans 7:24-25).

# CHAPTER ELEVEN

## Reach Out and Wrap Your Arms around Your Faith

SCRIPTURE: GENESIS 32:22-32

The woman sitting across the desk from me was crying softly and nervously twisting the dainty handkerchief she held in her hands. She was having trouble getting used to being a widow. Her husband had died less than a month ago. They had been married for more than thirty years. Her whole world had been wrapped up in him, and now he was gone. She was devastated and had come to the church for help. She admitted that she was having guilt feelings because she felt that she was not being strong. Well-meaning friends had inadvertently pushed her into a pretty severe guilt-trip. Over and over and over, they had said to her, "If you had more faith you wouldn't be taking this so hard."

The radio evangelist was preaching away at fever pitch. He was telling his listening audience that they needed to be saved. He was telling them in no uncertain terms that they were headed toward a terrible hell. "But," he added, "there is a way out. You can be saved. All you have to do is have faith."

The man on television was telling how God had spared his life. He was scheduled for a 7:30 p.m. flight but had a flat tire on the way to the airport. He missed the plane. The plane crashed and everyone on board was killed. The man said he knew that God had saved him because of his faith.

The news story told of a woman who had had a terrible terminal disease, but she had faith in God that she would be healed—and she was. "Now," she said to the reporter, "I tell people that, if they have a sickness, all they have to do is have enough faith in God and they will be healed!"

Recently, I heard two teenagers talking about one of their friends who used to come to church all the time, but not anymore. He had dropped out. He had gotten involved, they said, with the wrong crowd and evidently had lost his faith.

All of these vignettes obviously have to do with different understandings or misunderstandings of faith. *Faith*—what in the world is it?

*Faith* is a word we hear countless times. It's a word that rolls easily off the tongue, but what is it really? I read recently about a seminary professor who gave an interesting test. It had one question only: namely, "What is faith?" How would you have done on that test? What would you have put down? How would you define it? How would you describe it? How would you express it? How would you put it into words?

The truth is that that's a pretty hard test because *faith* is one of those words that we feel we know the meaning of until someone asks us to define it.

Now, there is a reason for that. Faith defies definition simply because it is an ongoing experience with God and is too big for words. Also, as we have already seen, there are many misunderstandings, distortions, half-truths, and differences of opinion about faith.

For instance, the friends telling the grieving widow that if she had more faith she wouldn't be taking it so hard meant well, but actually they were hurting and confusing her. I told her that that's like saying to me after I have hit my thumb with a hammer, "Now, don't cry." What do you mean "Don't cry!" It hurts! Faith can sustain us and encourage us and see us through dark valleys and tough times, but faith does not mean that we will feel no pain.

Or what about the radio preacher who says, "All you

need is faith"? What does that mean? What does it involve? How does it look and work in daily living? It's just not as simple as he makes it out to be.

Or how about the man on television saying his faith caused God to spare him from the plane crash? What about the people who went down with the plane? Didn't God love them too? Surely, some of them had faith, too.

Or the woman who said, "If you're sick, all you have to do is have faith, and you will be healed"? But, wait a minute, I want to say to her, I can think of hundreds of people who had tremendous faith who did not get healed—at least not in this lifetime. Even the Apostle Paul, with his great faith, never got relief from his "thorn in the flesh."

Then what about the two teenagers talking about their friend who had lost his faith? Can you do that? Is faith something you can find and then lose? We see clearly that there's much misunderstanding about faith, and for that reason I want to spend some time focusing in on faith, to help us understand what it is, what it's not, and how it works.

To get into this, I want to look at the life of Jacob. Here is a man who finally discovered what faith is after a long arduous struggle. It took him a long time—throughout his life he dabbled around with wrong conceptions of faith and wrong ideas about his relationships with God and with other people. Let's look quickly at his journey and see if we can find ourselves somewhere between the lines. I want to outline three stages of faith.

## First, Faith Is More Than a Family Affair

It is wonderful to have a great family, but that is not enough! Every person has to encounter the living Lord in his or her own unique way. We can ride on our family's coattails for just so long. Somewhere along the way, each of us has to discover our own personal relationship with God. Look at Jacob. He came from a strong religious family with a long religious heritage. Talk about a great heritage—Isaac, the great patriarch of Israel, was his father. Abraham, the father of the Jewish nation, was his grandfather. In his family, the name of God was respected and revered, prayer was commonplace, worship was regular, and faith was talked and lived daily.

But, at first, it didn't affect Jacob's way of living and dealing with others at all. If he had faith, it didn't spill over into his daily life. Remember how his brother Esau came in from hunting and he was starved. Jacob refused to share his food with his brother. What kind of faith is that? At least, he wouldn't share his food with his brother until they made a deal. "Give me your birthright and then you can have some of my food!"

What kind of faith is that? Then he tricked his blind father. He deceived him, lied to him, connived and plotted, and cheated away the blessing that should have gone to his brother, Esau. Jacob deceived his own father. He cheated his own brother. He lied, he plotted, he tricked, and he connived. What kind of faith is that? Jacob may have come from a religious family, but that's not enough. Jacob may have had a great religious heritage, but that's not enough. Jacob had heard all about God in his home, but he didn't really know God.

In Sunday school, a boy was asked why he believed in God. He answered: "I don't know for sure, but I think it runs in our family!" Now I know what that little boy was talking about—and I appreciate it—but really deep down, I wonder if he is completely correct. Our parents can influence us toward the Christian faith, to be sure, but they cannot do it *for* us! Faith is indeed something we share in the family and in the church and in our relations with all people, but ultimately it is also intensely *personal.* We are Christians, not by chromosomes, but finally only by our own conviction and commitment.

## Second, Faith Is More Than a Bargaining Affair

Faith is more than a "bargain basement deal," more than a "you scratch my back and I'll scratch yours" relationship with God and people. When Esau realized what Jacob had done, how he had tricked him and deceived him and their father, Esau was mad. Jacob skipped town. He ran away and came to a place called Bethel. There, for the first time, Jacob began to experience a real encounter with God.

He dreamed of a ladder stretching up all the way into the heavens. It was a symbol of the presence of God. God was there and available to Jacob. Jacob was ready. He was scared and in his fearful dilemma, Jacob was ready to deal with God. He tried to strike up a bargain: Now see here, Lord, he says, if you will be my God and watch over me (bargain number one), if you will keep me in my way (bargain number two), if you will give me food to eat (bargain number three), if you will give me clothes to wear (bargain number four), if you will bring me back to my father's house (bargain number five), then Lord, I'll let you be my God and I will serve you. Does any of that sound at all familiar? Jacob is telling God about the conditions of his discipleship. "Look here, Lord, if you will do all this for me, then I'll drop in to church every now and then, might even sing in the choir. If you measure up, Lord, if you'll do this for me, Lord, I might even go with the youth on their retreat." This is a tremendous illustration of what faith is *not*. It is not a bargaining, bartering relationship with God.

Remember the story about the multimillionaire on an airplane one morning, sitting next to a minister. All of a sudden the plane ran into a violent storm. It was being bounced around the sky like a toy. The millionaire got scared and he promised out loud, "God, if you'll get us down safely, I'll give you half of all that I own," which was a lot! Well, they made it through the storm and landed safely.

The minister reminded him of his promise: "I know you are ready to keep your bargain with God to give God half of all you own." The millionaire smiled and said, "Oh, that? As we were taxiing in, I made a better deal with God: If I ever got on an airplane again, God can have all of it!" He laughed and went merrily on his way, probably feeling that he had pulled a fast one on God.

Isn't that the way we do? The soldier in his trench saying, "Lord, get me home safely, and I will go to church every Sunday." The student at exam time saying, "Lord, help me pass this test, and I'll study next time, I promise." The executive promising, "Lord, get me that promotion, and I'll sing in the choir." The young ballplayer pleading, "Lord, let me hit a homerun, and I'll read my Sunday school lesson four weeks in a row."

That is not faith. That is presuming on God. It is

making God our celestial bellhop. It is telling God, "I will love you if you do what I ask," instead of telling God, "I will love you and serve you come what may."

### Finally, What Faith Really Is

It is more than a family affair; it is more than a bargaining affair. What is it? It is unconditional surrender to God. It's unflinching trust in God. It is unwavering commitment to God. Look at Jacob again. Twenty years have passed now, he has prospered, and he is coming home. His uncle Laban is chasing him because Jacob tricked him too, and Esau is coming out to meet him with four hundred men. Jacob is caught in the middle, between an angry uncle and a brother he betrayed. It was the "Dark Night of the Soul" for Jacob and on that dark night, he runs into God. There he wrestles with God. He struggles with who he is and what he has done. There he discovers what faith is. It is unconditional surrender to God. It is unwavering commitment to God. It is unflinching trust in God. It is unswerving allegiance to God.

I recently ran across a poignant Eastern legend that makes the point well. The legend tells of a young man pledging his undying love to his girlfriend. "I love you more than anything," he says. "I love you more than life itself," he says. "My love for you is rock-solid and certain," he says. "You are the only one for me," he says. "Oh no!" says the girl sweetly, "I think you would much prefer my sister in the next room. She is so much more beautiful than I am." The man went into the next room to check this out. Moments later he returned and said: "You tricked me. Your sister is not nearly as beautiful as you." "No," said the girl, "it is you who almost tricked me, for if you had really loved me as you had said you did, you never would have gone into the next room to look!" Real faith is unwavering, unswerving commitment to God.

It is Job in agony crying out: "Though he slay me, yet will I trust in him" (13:15 KJV). It is Shadrach, Meshach, and Abednego trapped in the fiery furnace shouting to King Nebuchadnezzar: "If our God whom we serve is able to deliver us from the furnace of blazing fire . . . let him deliver us. But if not . . . we will not serve your gods and we will not worship the golden statue that you have set up" (Daniel 3:17-18). It is Luther in big trouble saying, "Here I stand . . . I can do no other! God help me!" It is Bonhoeffer in the horrible existence of a prison camp praying each morning, "Lord, whatever this day may bring . . . Thy Name be praised!" It is Jesus in the Garden of Gethsemane: "Father, if you are willing, remove this cup from me; yet, not my will but yours be done" (Luke 22:42).

Let me ask you something: Do you have a faith like that? Do you have a faith that is unshakeable, unflinching, unswerving, and unwavering? Faith—what in the world is it? Simply this: it is unconditional surrender to God! It is unflinching trust in God! It is unbending commitment to God!

# CHAPTER TWELVE

## Reach Out and Wrap Your Arms around What Christ Gives to Us

SCRIPTURE: LUKE 19:1-10

Some years ago a little-known play entitled *Closed Because of Death* played off-Broadway in New York City. In the play, history comes to an end. Everybody dies. The earth is barren and seemingly the symbol of defeat. But in the last act, the scene shifts to heaven. God is sitting there staring off into the future. He is holding a baby on his lap. Two angels pass by. One turns and says to the other, "He isn't going to start over again is he? Doesn't he ever learn?" The second angel answers: "Well, you see, that is precisely the difference between God and us. God always sees a chance to start all over again!" That is, indeed, the good news of our faith, isn't it? And that is what the story of Zacchaeus is all about: the chance—with God's help—to start all over again.

We Americans place a great emphasis on starting out on something. We make a big deal over starting out in a new position, a new marriage, a new career, or even a new house. There is something very exciting about starting out on those first few steps of a new journey. However, the truth is that some of life's greatest moments come, not when we start out, but when we start over.

Some years ago, I heard about a number of people who had one thing in common: They were all starting over. There was a middle-aged wife and mother who had dropped out of college to have a family. Now, with her children grown and with her husband encouraging her, she was starting over again. A nervous but determined fifty-year-old college sophomore—what a beautiful sight!

There was a man in his mid-thirties who had lost himself in every conceivable way the last few years. But now, with a new job, a new self-respect, and a new marriage to "an angel disguised as a woman" (to use his words) he was starting out again as fresh as a newborn child—what a beautiful sight!

Then, there was a ministerial colleague in his seventies who talked of the richness of retirement in one moment, and his call to the ministry in another. His formal career was over, but he was preparing to take up his ministry again. He had all the enthusiasm of a newly ordained elder, but all the wisdom and maturity of a seasoned veteran. It was a long time ago that he started out serving the church, but in just a few weeks, he was starting over again. A retired cleric who is not retiring—what a beautiful sight!

Perhaps the greatest teaching of Christianity is that it is never too late to start over again. God's love forever offers us new dreams, and God's power gives us the strength to turn them into reality. No matter how old we are, how far we have traveled, or how many mistakes we have made, it is never too late to start over again. Why is this? Because God has more life in store for us tomorrow than we have been able to find today.

That's why we like the Zacchaeus story so much. Jesus' encounter with Zacchaeus is the dramatic picture of how God can turn our lives around and give us a new beginning. This story is one of the most loved and best-known stories in the Bible and also one of the most revealing. It is found only in the Gospel of Luke—not in Matthew, Mark, or John—and that in itself is significant.

We remember from our study of the New Testament that each of the Gospel writers had a dominant theme or a unique emphasis. For example, Matthew is the Jewish Gospel, showing how Jesus is the long-awaited Messiah predicted by the Old Testament. Mark, on the other hand, is written crisply like an Alfred Hitchcock thriller. It is written to a people under persecution, and it shows how Jesus himself faced harsh, brutal, and undeserved persecution yet was victorious over it. Then John is written for the philosophical mind, showing how Jesus was the "Word made flesh," the truth of God wrapped up in a person.

Now, the Gospel of Luke has an entirely different dimension altogether. It was written around 89 to 95 A.D. by a Gentile physician—a kind of welfare doctor—and it is dedicated uniquely to the down and outs, the losers, the outcasts of life. As a matter of fact, one of the verses here in the Zacchaeus story (19:10) reads, "the Son of Man came to seek out and to save the lost." Many Bible scholars underscore that one sentence as the basic theme of the entire Gospel of Luke. All through Luke, we see it, story after story where Jesus is helping the needy, reaching out to the untouchables, caring for the unloved, lifting up the lowly. Think of it, the prodigal son, the good Samaritan, the ten lepers, the Pharisee and the publican, the penitent thief on the cross, Jesus' prayer for the Roman soldiers ("Father, forgive them"), the Zacchaeus encounter—these stories all have surprise endings where an outcast comes out on top, and they are all found only in Luke—not in Matthew, Mark, or John—only in Luke!

Luke's Gospel sees in Jesus a special and gracious love for the lowly and rejected outcasts of life. Those no one else cared for, Jesus loved, embraced, and accepted in a touching way. Luke, the welfare doctor, liked that about Jesus and he wrote it large in his Gospel. We see it graphically here as Jesus reaches out to Zacchaeus.

Jesus came into Jericho, the City of Palms. A great parade applauded his arrival. People lined the streets in huge numbers. We can just imagine that the mayor and the city council were there with a key to the city, and the established church leaders were there to check out this traveling preacher who was causing such a stir. Everybody was there. Some were believers; some were there out of curiosity. Businesses were shut down. Schools were closed. Household chores were set aside. Everybody turned out—all of them on the streets lining the way.

But they weren't *all* along the street. One of them was up in a tree. His name was Zacchaeus. He was a tax collector and a dishonest one at that. If they had conducted a popularity contest in Jericho that day, Zacchaeus may well have come in dead last. He was a short man, and short people sometimes have to be creative to see over a crowd. So he rose to the occasion by climbing a sycamore tree.

As Jesus came into the city, he began to look at the faces in the crowd. His eyes found Zacchaeus perched up in that tree, the picture of loneliness and rejection, the outcast of outcasts, the lowest of the lowly. And the heart of Jesus was touched. He walked over, looked up, and said: "Zacchaeus, come down quickly! Let's have lunch together." Now notice verse 7. It reads like this: "All who saw it began to grumble." That may be one of the most understated verses in the Bible. You can bet there was a grumble! The city fathers were there. The leading citizens were there. The prominent business executives were there. The pillars of the church were there. And instead of having lunch with any of them, of all things, Jesus goes to lunch with the number one crook in town!

Now, at this point in the story, there is a blank spot. We don't know what happened at lunch, we don't know what was said at Zacchaeus's home, and we don't know what transpired over the meal. All we know is that Zacchaeus came out a changed man, a penitent man, a man ready to make amends, a man ready to start over and do better. "Look, half of my possessions, Lord, I will give to the poor; and if I have defrauded anyone of anything, I will pay back four times as much" (v. 8). Talk about conversion! I mean, he was converted! His soul was touched. His heart was warmed and even his pocketbook got converted!

In this amazing story, we see dramatically the power of God's redeeming love, a love that has the strength to absolutely turn our lives around. In this incredible story as Zacchaeus is converted, we see the generous gifts God so graciously gives to us through Jesus Christ our Lord. They are so magnificent and so numerous. Let me underscore three of them.

## First, There Is the Gift of Acceptance

Jesus accepted Zacchaeus and challenged him to be better. There is a moving scene in Bel Kaufman's novel *Up the Down Staircase* involving a young teacher whose first assignment was in a tough New York City high school. The book tells about her difficulties and frustrations in getting close to the students, most of whom come from very troubled and impoverished backgrounds.

One day she puts a small suggestion box on her desk and tells the students that if there is anything they want to tell her, they can write it on a slip of paper and leave it in the box. A few days later she finds a message in the box. It's written by a young boy who, when he's in school at all, sits in the back corner of the classroom—

hostile, sullen, uncooperative—seemingly at odds with the teacher and everyone. He has scrawled on a piece of paper these words: "I wish you knew who I was!"

We all do. We need the recognition, the touch, the attention, and the acceptance of people around us in order to give meaning and hope to life. If we are cut off from other people, out of touch, rejected, or despised, it can be a living death. Some years ago, Mother Teresa, reflecting on her experiences in life, indicated that she had discovered that the worst disease in the world is not leprosy or cancer or TB, but rather being unwanted.

You can work miracles if you're willing to give the gift of acceptance. Jesus knew that. He accepted Zacchaeus. He included Zacchaeus. He reached out to Zacchaeus, and he changed Zacchaeus's life! Christ gives to us the gift of acceptance, and he wants us to pass that gift on to others.

## Second, There Is the Gift of Forgiveness

Jesus knew about Zacchaeus. He called him by name. He knew about his checkered past, and he gave him what he needed most at that moment—forgiveness!

Several years ago, I gave a book review at our church for the United Methodist Women Book Club. I shared a personal experience I had never talked about publicly before, at least to that extent. Afterwards, a lady in that group, whose judgment I respect greatly, told me that I should tell that story publicly, so here it is.

I have shared the story before of how I lost my father in an automobile accident when I was twelve years old. It happened on a Sunday afternoon. My dad had appendicitis. He was in great pain. We couldn't get an ambulance, so our neighbor from across the street agreed to take him to the hospital in our car. My dad was in the back seat, lying down with his head in mother's lap when the accident occurred. All the people involved in the wreck were seriously hurt. As they were brought into the emergency room at Methodist Hospital in Memphis, the chaplain, who had formerly been our pastor, recognized my parents. He came to our home to tell us about the accident and to take us back to the hospital.

My brother, who was fourteen, my six-year-old sister, my grandmother, and I walked the floor, prayed, and waited for some word. Finally, we were told to go on home for the night and come back tomorrow. So we went home and went to bed. Shortly after we had fallen to sleep, the call came that my father had died. The relatives, who had gathered in by this time, decided to let the children sleep and to tell us in the morning. But there was something they didn't count on. I got up early and went out to get the morning paper, and there on the front page of the *Memphis Commercial Appeal* was the picture of our smashed-up car with a caption that read "Wendell Moore killed in car wreck."

As I think of myself sitting there in our living room with the newspaper on my lap, looking at that picture of our smashed-up car and that news story, I remember two things vividly. First, I remember feeling sorry for my relatives as one by one they came in and saw me sitting there and didn't know what to say. Also, I remember feeling so guilty. A few months before at a family picnic, I was showing off with a baseball, threw it wildly, hit my dad in the hand, and broke his thumb. He walked the floor all night in agony with that broken thumb. When I read about my father's death, I thought of that and felt so guilty. "What a terrible son I had been! I broke my dad's thumb and caused him great pain, and I wasn't sure that I had adequately said: 'I'm sorry.' " I lived with that guilt in silence for several weeks.

Finally, some months after the funeral—I still can't believe I did this at twelve years of age—I called the church and made an appointment with my pastor. When I told him what I was worrying about, he was so great! He handled it so beautifully. He walked around the desk with big tears streaming down his cheeks. He was an older man. He sat down in front of me and said: "Now, Jim, listen to me. If your dad could come back to life for five minutes and be with us here in this office right now, and if he knew you were worrying about that, what would he say to you?"

I said, "He would tell me he loves me and it's OK and to stop worrying about that."

"That's exactly right," said my minister, "so you stop worrying about that right now."

And I did because that minister gave me what I needed—the assurance of forgiveness!

That's what Christ did for Zacchaeus, and that is the special gift he has for each one of us, the gift of forgiveness. He gives to us the gift of forgiveness and wants us to live in that spirit and to pass it on to others.

### Finally, There Is the Gift of Life

In Scotland there is a lighthouse called Old William's Light. The man who kept that light would come into town two times a week to get groceries and to go to church. But one day, he did not show up at his regular time. There had been a bad storm the night before, so his friends were worried about him. They went over to the lighthouse and found him there unconscious. He had slipped on the rocks and had broken his leg. But somehow he knew that the light needed to be lit that night. So he had agonizingly crawled up those long spiral stairs to the top in order to turn on the light.

Because of his weakened condition he caught pneumonia and later died in the hospital. After his funeral, a man came and said, "I want to erect a monument to this light keeper. I was the captain of a ship and was caught in the storm that night. I did not know where I was and was headed for the rocks. Then the light came on and I was able to see." Then he said, "This is the first time in my life I can truly say somebody died that I might live."

He was wrong, of course. Because two thousand years ago on a hill called Calvary, Christ died so that we could live. He preached love, he stood tall for what is right, and then he climbed up on a cross for you and me, to die that we might live. The Son of Man came to seek and save the lost, to give us acceptance, forgiveness, and life.

# DISCUSSION GUIDE

for
*Do You Have Alligator Arms?*

BY JAMES W. MOORE

JOHN D. SCHROEDER

## 1. Do You Have Alligator Arms?

### Snapshot Summary

This chapter defines the term *alligator arms* and explores why people often fail to reach out and make a full commitment to opportunities they encounter.

### Reflection / Discussion Questions

1. What does the term *alligator arms* mean? Give an example of it.
2. What attitudes or reasoning often prevent people from making a commitment and paying the price?
3. Share a time when you lacked commitment and had an "alligator arms" attitude.

4. Name some common opportunities missed because of having alligator arms.
5. What lessons can be learned from the encounter of Jesus and the Rich Young Ruler?
6. Why is it important not to hesitate in telling someone you love him or her?
7. Why do some people hesitate to say they are sorry?
8. Share a time when you said you were sorry to someone. How did you feel? How did that person respond?
9. Give some reasons why we need to say "yes" to Christ now, not later.
10. What additional thoughts or questions from this chapter would you like to explore?

#### Activities

*As a group:* Make your own personal commitment card that says what you are going to do this week to show you do not have alligator arms. Share your commitment with the group.

*At home:* Examine areas of your life where you may be lacking in commitment and where you need to begin reaching out.

Prayer: *Dear God, thank you for warning us not to miss opportunities to serve you and others. Help us reach out to those in need, showing faith and commitment. Amen.*

## 2. Reach Out and Wrap Your Arms around God's Future

#### Snapshot Summary

This chapter offers encouragement to create new beginnings, as a person of faith and as a believer in God and in the future.

**Reflection / Discussion Questions**

1. Share a difficult time in your life when you eagerly sought a fresh start or new beginning.
2. Reflect on / discuss why tomorrow is a precious gift.
3. Describe some of the different ways some people approach the future.
4. Why is the future or change so scary for some people?
5. Name some of the advantages of approaching the future as believers.
6. What does it mean to be a believer? Explain it in your own words.
7. Reflect on / discuss how we "believe the future in" and how the Apostle Paul helps us.
8. What does it mean to be a person of faith? Why is faith so important?
9. Describe the roles hope and love play in "believing the future in."
10. What additional thoughts or questions from this chapter would you like to explore?

**Activities**

*As a group:* Ask each member to draw a symbol representing God's future. Share and discuss your symbols. Or let each member create seven one-word personal affirmations using the letters of the word *believe*. Share your seven affirmations with one another.

*At home:* Look into your future. What role does God play in it? What are your goals?

Prayer: *Dear God, thank you that we have a future with you. Help us grow in faith and be true believers, always ready to serve you and others. Amen.*

# 3. Reach Out and Wrap Your Arms around Trust in God

### Snapshot Summary

This chapter encourages us to trust in God, not to hold grudges, and to put our lives in God's hands.

### Reflection / Discussion Questions

1. In your own words, what does it mean to trust in God?
2. Share a time when you put your trust in God during a challenging situation.
3. What can we learn from Paul's letter to the Ephesians?
4. List some things we have little or no control over that have to be left to God.
5. Reflect on / discuss what happens when we entrust God with our hurts and pains.
6. Why is bearing grudges or seeking revenge never productive or wise?
7. Give an example of how God took a personal defeat or failure and used it for good.
8. Reflect on / discuss why we can entrust to God our future. How is this done?
9. What costs and benefits are there in trusting in God?
10. What additional thoughts or questions from this chapter would you like to explore?

### Activities

*As a group:* Write down five reasons each why you trust God. Share your reasons with the group.

*At home:* Do a trust inventory on who you trust, and why. Examine your trust in God. Think and pray about how to strengthen your trust.

Prayer: *Dear God, thank you for giving us opportunities to trust you and to stretch our faith. Help us not doubt or hold back, but move forward with trust in you. Amen.*

## 4. Reach Out and Wrap Your Arms around Jesus and His Message

### Snapshot Summary

This chapter examines the message of Jesus and why Judas missed the message and betrayed Jesus.

### Reflection / Discussion Questions

1. What mandate did Judas miss?
2. Share a time when you listened to someone's story and then felt differently toward that person.
3. Name some different ways of reaching out to Jesus.
4. Why is it natural to seek simple explanations to complex problems?
5. Reflect on / discuss how Judas is often portrayed, and why.
6. Reflect on / discuss some of the possible reasons why Judas betrayed Jesus.
7. What can we learn from the life of Judas?
8. How did Judas miss the message? How do we sometimes also miss the message?
9. What key moments did Judas miss?
10. What additional thoughts or questions from this chapter would you like to explore?

### Activities

*As a group:* Use the Bible to locate and list adjectives that describe Judas.

*At home:* Take a close look at yourself. Are you missing the message of Jesus or are you being receptive to it?

Prayer: *Dear God, thank you for being patient with us as we often miss or forget your message. Remind us to love others, help those in need, and live according to your word. Amen.*

## 5. Reach Out and Wrap Your Arms around a Sense of Purpose, Trust, and Love

### Snapshot Summary

This chapter shows how distorted values can interfere with maintaining a sense of purpose, trust, and love. It also uses advice from the Apostle Paul to help us with values and purpose.

### Reflection / Discussion Questions

1. Share a time when you struggled to find a sense of purpose, trust, or love.
2. Give some examples of how society confuses and distorts our values.
3. Reflect on / discuss the damage caused by distorted values.
4. Is it helpful to look for who is to blame for creating distorted values and priorities? Explain your answer.
5. In Philippians 4, what does Paul say about values?
6. What makes Philippians 4:13 one of the greatest verses in the Bible? Why is it so powerful?
7. Talk about the importance of having a sacred sense of purpose.
8. Give some examples of how Jesus demonstrated total trust in God.
9. Describe some simple ways we can spread "love-energy" in our world.
10. What additional thoughts or questions from this chapter would you like to explore?

### Activities

*As a group:* Let each member create a brief prayer based upon this lesson. Share your prayers.

*At home:* This week, focus on purpose, trust, and love. How can you improve in these areas? How is your relationship with God?

Prayer: *Dear God, thank you for demonstrating what it means to have a sense of purpose, trust, and love. Help us escape from the trap of distorted values and live for you alone. Amen.*

## 6. Reach Out and Wrap Your Arms around the Hunger for Righteousness

### Snapshot Summary

This chapter uses the fourth Beatitude to examine personal goodness and how we can stand tall for social justice.

### Reflection / Discussion Questions

1. Explain what it means to hunger for righteousness.
2. Share a time when you were fired up in a pursuit of goodness and righteousness.
3. Reflect on / discuss the meaning of the fourth Beatitude.
4. How do you develop real passion and commitment? How is this hunger born?
5. Name some ways we can increase our desire for goodness.
6. How did Jesus practice righteousness in his life?
7. Explain what is meant by "personal goodness."
8. Name some ways we can stand tall for social justice.
9. How are we set right with God and others?
10. What additional thoughts or questions from this chapter would you like to explore?

### Activities

*As a group:* Let each member create a menu for those who hunger for righteousness. List the ingredients or the different courses of a satisfying meal. Share your menus with one another.

*At home:* Make righteousness your theme or keyword this week. Take some action steps in the direction of goodness.

Prayer: *Dear God, thank you for giving us a hunger for righteousness and for demonstrating the meaning of goodness. Help us develop a real hunger, passion, and commitment for goodness. Amen.*

## 7. Reach Out and Wrap Your Arms around Spiritual Maturity

### Snapshot Summary

This chapter uses the topics of rejection, hostility, and lashing out to examine the meaning of spiritual maturity.

### Reflection / Discussion Questions

1. In your own words, what does it mean to be spiritually mature?
2. Reflect on / discuss some ways in which Jesus demonstrated spiritual maturity.
3. What are some signs that a person is spiritually mature—what evidence should we expect?
4. How should we respond when faced with hostility?
5. Give some reasons why we tend to take things personally.
6. Name some reasons why we should not take things personally.
7. Share a time when you experienced rejection and describe how you felt.

8. Reflect on / discuss the three options the author lists for responding to people who lash out at us.
9. Describe some ways we can gain spiritual maturity.
10. What additional thoughts or questions from this chapter would you like to explore?

**Activities**

*As a group:* Explore the books of Psalms and Proverbs for advice about spiritual maturity. Let each member of the group offer some biblical wisdom from these two books.

*At home:* Focus on spiritual maturity this week. Are you mature and growing in your faith? How can you improve?

Prayer: *Dear God, thank you for reminding us of the importance of spiritual maturity and how to wrap our arms around it. Help us not take things so personally, and in all situations help us respond as Jesus would respond. Amen.*

## 8. Reach Out and Wrap Your Arms around the Spirit of Compassion

**Snapshot Summary**

This chapter calls us to be compassionate people and reminds us how simple acts of compassion can change lives.

**Reflection / Discussion Questions**

1. Share a time when you received or offered compassion.
2. List some of the benefits of being a compassionate person.
3. Reflect on / discuss why the author calls compassion "God's most important lesson."
4. Why do you think some people lack compassion?
5. Who modeled compassion for you when you were growing up?

6. Reflect on / discuss the element of sensitivity in compassion. Why is it important?
7. How and why does compassion work with interruptions? Give an example.
8. Describe how Jesus modeled gracious compassion during his ministry.
9. Name some simple acts of compassion that are examples of love in action.
10. What additional thoughts or questions from this chapter would you like to explore?

### Activities

*As a group:* Make a list of ten different acts of compassion that are simple to perform. Together, make a commitment to doing these simple acts of compassion.

*At home:* Use your Bible this week to explore acts of compassion. Use your words and deeds this week to show the true meaning of compassion.

Prayer: *Dear God, thank you for reminding us how important it is to be compassionate toward one another. Help us look for opportunities to reach out to others in a spirit of caring, as givers of God's love. Amen.*

## 9. Reach Out and Wrap Your Arms around Your Christian Witness

### Snapshot Summary

This chapter uses the story of *Through the Valley of the Kwai* to show what it means to be a witness for Christ and how to share your faith redemptively.

### Reflection / Discussion Questions

1. What impressed you about the story of *Through the Valley of the Kwai* as described by the author?

2. Reflect on / discuss what it means to be an ambassador for Christ.
3. When you hear the word *witness*, what images or words come to mind?
4. Reflect on / discuss how well most Christians represent God; include in your assessment both strengths and weaknesses.
5. What does it mean to reverently share your faith? How is this done?
6. Why is respect for people so important for Christian witness?
7. Give some possible examples of a relevant Christian witness.
8. What does it mean to share your faith redemptively?
9. Name some simple ways of effectively sharing your faith.
10. What additional thoughts or questions from this chapter would you like to explore?

**Activities**

*As a group:* Search the New Testament for examples of effective witness. How did the disciples do it? What can we learn from them?

*At home:* Act like a witness this week. Focus on your speech and actions. Pray about becoming a more effective witness for Christ.

Prayer: *Dear God, thank you for encouraging us to reach out and wrap our arms around others as Christian witnesses. Help us be both relevant and redemptive as we share our faith with others. Amen.*

## 10. Reach Out and Wrap Your Arms around Your Christian Conscience

**Snapshot Summary**

This chapter examines the need for us to make ethical decisions, and it offers some guidelines and examples.

### Reflection / Discussion Questions

1. Share a time when you had to make an ethical decision.
2. Why is it often so hard to make an ethical decision? What factors come into play?
3. Reflect on / discuss the pros and cons of having your conscience be your guide.
4. How can a conscience be tricked or corrupted?
5. What role can prayer play in making an ethical decision?
6. Talk about ways to cultivate a Christian conscience.
7. Name the key to a Christian conscience. Why is this important?
8. Share how you personally go about telling right from wrong.
9. When we think we know what is right, why can we still have trouble doing it?
10. What additional thoughts or questions from this chapter would you like to explore?

### Activities

*As a group:* Let each member create on paper his or her own version of a "Jesus Measuring Stick" that can be used to help make ethical decisions. Share your creations.

*At home:* Ask yourself if are you an ethical person. Examine your conscience, and pray about being ethical in all your acts and decisions.

Prayer: *Dear God, thank you for reminding us of the choice between right and wrong. Help us make ethical decisions. Amen.*

## 11. Reach Out and Wrap Your Arms around Your Faith

### Snapshot Summary

This chapter uses the life of Jacob to show us truths about faith and how we can strengthen our belief in God.

### Reflection / Discussion Questions

1. In your own words, what is faith? What does it mean to have faith?
2. Why is it so hard to define or express faith?
3. Describe some of the misunderstandings about faith.
4. What confuses you the most about faith or having faith?
5. Can you lose faith? If so, can you find it again?
6. Reflect on / discuss why faith is more than a family affair.
7. Why is faith more than a bargaining affair?
8. Reflect on / discuss "what faith really is," as described by the author.
9. What lessons can we learn from Jacob about faith?
10. What additional thoughts or questions from this chapter would you like to explore?

### Activities

*As a group:* Use a hymnal to explore different aspects and meanings of faith. How is faith expressed in music? What hymns or songs inspire you in your faith?

*At home:* Examine your faith. Can you express your faith? How can you strengthen your faith?

Prayer: *Dear God, thank you for reminding us of the importance of having a real and living faith. Help us nurture our faith through prayer, reading the Bible, and sharing our faith with others. Amen.*

## 12. Reach Out and Wrap Your Arms around What Christ Gives to Us

### Snapshot Summary

This chapter looks at the gifts Christ gives us, including acceptance, forgiveness, and life itself, and it reminds us that we can start over.

### Reflection / Discussion Questions

1. Share a time when you started over. How did it feel?
2. List some of the pros and cons of starting over.
3. Describe some of the times or situations in which people are forced to begin again.
4. What lessons can we learn about new beginnings from the encounter of Zacchaeus and Jesus?
5. Christ gives us the gift of acceptance. How can we pass that gift on to others?
6. What do we need to do to receive the gift of forgiveness?
7. Why can we be assured of forgiveness by God?
8. What makes the gift of life so precious?
9. We are so blessed by gifts from God. How can we pass these gifts on to others?
10. What additional thoughts or questions from this chapter would you like to explore?

### Activities

*As a group:* Celebrate the completion of your small-group experience with a graduation party.

*At home:* Reflect upon your reading, reflection, and discussion of this book. What have you learned? What would you like to change in your life?

Prayer: *Dear God, thank you for all the gifts you so generously provide. Thank you especially for this small-group experience. Help us remember and apply what we have learned from this book and from our time with one another. Amen.*